C000097328

*S*peak

Fluent Man

The Top Things Women Should Consider
Before Blaming The Man

Von Decarlo

B.B.P.

Copyright ©™ Von Decarlo 2014, 2015

The right of Von Decarlo to be identified as the author
of this work has been asserted by her in accordance with
the Copyright, Designs and Patents Act 1988 (or other
similar law, depending on your country).

All rights reserved
Printed in the United States of America

No part of this book may be reproduced, stored in a
retrieval system, or transmitted, in any form, or by any
means (electronic, mechanical, photocopying, recording
or otherwise) without the prior written permission of
Von Decarlo, except in cases of brief quotations
embodied in reviews or articles. It may not be edited,
amended, lent, resold, hired out, distributed or otherwise
circulated without the publisher's written permission.
Permission can be obtained from SpeakFluentMan.com

ISBN: 9781631928062

Published by
Von Decarlo
Buttercup Brown Publishing, LLC. 2015 B.B.P.
All Rights Reserved

Edited by
Von Decarlo and Kay Busby

Copy Edited by
Nick First

Cover Photo by
Marco Castaneda

About The Author by
Sansan Fibri

To MiMi

One day, it will all make sense. Thank you for being born.
You saved my life.

ACKNOWLEDGEMENTS

Many people have supported me in writing and developing this book, both personally and professionally.

Many thanks to Kay Busby for her faith in this book as well as her faith in me as a person. Your friendship has gotten me through many dark moments, many of which we shared in developing this book.

To the wonderful ensemble of special people associated with Patrice whose collective love and support has enabled me to dedicate the time and focus needed to write this book, I extend a lifetime of gratitude to you. I would like to specifically acknowledge Greg "Opie" Hughes, Jim Norton, Anthony Cumia, and Bill Burr for being on the forefront of that support.

To Jason Steinberg, my manager who when few people would consider working with me independently of my association with Patrice, you did. Thank you for believing in my individual talents as an artist.

And lastly, to my dear mother, Joyce Brown who told me when I was a child that I could do anything I set my mind to if I would just believe. I believed you then, and I believe you now.

Special Acknowledgement & Thank You
The Stand Restaurant & Comedy Club
Love Logan Productions
Adrian LeBlanc

All Glory to God

Contents

Introduction

"I don't have jokes, I have soliloquies."

— Patrice O'Neal

INTRODUCTION

I was fortunate enough to be blessed as the chosen one to spend ten intimate years with a man that many considered a genius. In fact, many people considered comedian Patrice O'Neal a genius long before he passed away. When a person dies, often times we see people hop on the bandwagon of praise in which the term genius is overused. However, when Patrice passed away, the honest and true effect he had on people and their lives resonated loudly in their humble, truth-filled statements. Most of what his friends, family, fans, and even enemies were saying was very consistent with what they said about him when he was alive. From expressions of intense loss and sadness, to jokes about having to buy a "large casket and a shiny purple suit," the overwhelming response from people was legitimately honest, just as Patrice would have expected and liked. There were so many mentionable declarations from so many people, but the one statement that many thought I should be utterly offended by was the one made by Patrice's nemesis, Comedian Lisa Lampanelli.

Lisa stated that she did not like Patrice when he was here, and continued with a rhetorical question, asking, "Am I supposed to pretend to like him now because he's dead?" When I first heard about Lisa Lampanelli's statement, the first thing I did was smile. I looked up to heaven in hopes of connecting to Patrice in spirit just to acknowledge him once again as the epitome of truth. It never ceased to amaze me how much Patrice inspired courage and honesty in so many people, even those who did not like or agree with him much. Now, I dare not say that Lisa would not have had the courage to make such a bold, honest statement about a person's passing except for that it was Patrice, and she knew what he stood for; but it is certainly fair to assume that is why she felt comfortable in doing so. While many people may have thought that her expression of Patrice's passing was insensitive, I embraced it with a smile and respect for an expression of truth, just as I am one hundred percent sure Patrice would have embraced it in the same way. I am certain that he would not have been mad at her, so how could I dare be angry? In fact, if she would have said anything different, he may have come back to life just to lecture her on the importance of being honest. I am sure if he were here to respond to Lisa's truth-filled statement, he would have just condescendingly patted her on top of the head and said, *"Good girl,"* because at all costs, Patrice O'Neal embraced honesty.

Whether or not you have ever met Patrice and spent personal time with him, most people generally know that he was a fan and protector of the freedom to express your personal truth, even if he disagreed with you. He was always up for a good debate, but he would never discourage someone to lie and agree just because of fear of some type of repercussion. Patrice truly believed in freedom of speech and felt so committed to protecting his right to be able to say whatever he wanted that, unlike most, he lived by the principal of equality and protected

that right to speak the truth for all—even if that truth was

against him. He once explained that the cost to keep your

own freedom of speech is to be obligated to defend

others for that same right whether you agree with them

or not—even if their honesty is against you. Seems like

common sense, but in the grand scheme of things, most

people really only take interest in defending their own

personal right to free expression and the rights of others

who agree with them. However, Patrice understood on

another level that disagreeing with someone does not

overrule their right to express what they believe and feel.

You can debate about it, but you cannot shut down their

right to express. He always encouraged people to live in

their truth regardless of probable consequences, and he

led by example in how he lived his life, both personally

and professionally. He called this concept of

courageously living in your personal truth

"righteousness."

"I'm here to speak for funny." — *Patrice O'Neal*

One of Patrice's best moments in defending the right to be *righteous* was on Fox News, when he was the first person to speak out in defense of comedic talk radio host Don Imus when he was fired as a result of his controversial "nappy headed hoe" comment, while at the same time defending his radio buddies, Opie and Anthony, for their infamous Condoleezza Rice rape joke made by a homeless man live on their radio show. Patrice's stance on Fox News was that he was speaking out not necessarily in agreement or disagreement with any of the statements or "jokes" made, but that he was defending the right for one *to attempt* to be funny. Arguing the point that *"funny and unfunny jokes are birthed from the same place,"* he went so far as to point out the fact that not many rape jokes are likely to result in an *actual* rape (especially the rape of a prominent political figure), which illustrated the lack of respect that some people have for context in speech, especially in comedy. He also pointed out to me earlier that day before going into the Fox studios that the origin of Don Imus' poorly delivered nappy headed hoe comment was derived from the classic Spike Lee movie *School Daze*, emphasizing to me the double standards that exist in the freedom to express when race is involved. He was intent on making people understand the double standards that existed in racial speech (especially between black and white Americans). It may feel offensive to hear a person of a different race say certain things that we find humorous when it comes from someone of our same background, but true equality is the right for anyone to be able to say it, regardless of how you feel. He also felt that if we as black people continued to contribute to the shutdown of a white person's freedom to say whatever they want because we are unequally offended, then eventually they would find a way to shut black people down as well and/or neutralize the playing field. To further reveal his point to me, he gave a specific example, pointing out the fact that he hadn't heard the word nigger, or nigga, in his entire life from a white person as much as he constantly, almost on a daily basis, heard the phrase "n-word" on the news and in everyday casual conversations, since it had been adopted as acceptable. But, aside from the specific racial issues, he also felt that overall, the "powers that be" in America were finding a way to neutralize double standards in language and speech in general through fear tactics of being fired and/or blacklisted, thereby slowly taking away freedom of speech from all of us in general.

Patrice undoubtedly had an uncanny, out of the box way of thinking, and the ability to translate what others would consider a complicated situation into a very matter of fact, simple, elementary point, inspiring many people—close friends, family, and fans—to be amazed at his soliloquies. He could wrap up an entire point and debate in one sentence and leave a person wondering why they had not thought of it themselves. He was looked upon as the go-to guy for interpretation of many life situations, from pop culture, politics, race relations, conspiracy theories, music, sports, and of course, his favorite subject of them all, love, relationships, and women.

Patrice's journey to finding his place with women started at a very young age, as with most men. I cannot give you all of the details of his personal dealings with women on his journey to develop his amazing philosophies. I can only share the ones that he shared with me as examples to help me grow as a woman and become what he eventually considered his "top trained soldier." He was proud of my development and my ability to grasp and apply his concepts and expressed on many occasions publically that I possess what he called a "black belt in Patrice." He also said that I have a lot to share and offer because he noticed that most females listened to his philosophies differently when they heard them come from me, a fellow woman. As a result, he suggested (a couple of years before his passing) that I write a book on his philosophies from my perspective, sharing all that I had learned from him in building a solid, successful, loving relationship. Reluctant at first, I shied away from the idea of writing a book. I felt very insecure about expressing and sharing all that I had learned in my relationship with Patrice because I knew it would come with a certain amount of scrutiny and debate, and I was honestly not interested in taking that level of debate upon myself. At the time, I was unsure that I could handle the hostility that I was certain to encounter from people who disagreed with such philosophies. Not that I did not believe in the philosophies enough to write about them and defend my stance, but to me, debating just seemed like a vicious sport where most people only listen long enough to dissect what you are saying—just to figure out a way to make you wrong and themselves right. Patrice loved the sport of debate and the challenge of changing peoples' minds. He never lost patience or energy in any debate, whereas, I just did not care to have that kind of patience with opposition or aggression. While I do not mind sharing and teaching, I am really only interested in doing so with a person that has an open heart and mind, not someone looking for a reason to argue and fight until I break them down with truth.

On many occasions, people (mostly women) in their efforts to argue against Patrice's philosophies, have called me dumb, gullible, and brainwashed. One time, after one of Patrice's comedy shows, a woman approached me, patted me on the back, and said she felt sorry for me. As I smiled and kindly placed my hand on her shoulder, my retort was "Why? I am happy. In fact, I feel sorry for you and the lie you and your husband must live because I know if you're that comfortable judging me and you don't even know me, you must torture him with condemnation," referring to her husband standing next to her at the time. Now, I was not necessarily being defensive or condescending, nor did I say that to her in a nasty way. I was simply being honest about the fact that I was truly happy in my relationship by way of living in truth and acceptance, exactly as Patrice had described for an hour and a half on stage. Her attitude, on the other hand, was that of a very critical, narrow-minded individual that seemed to prefer living a lie with her husband in order to appease her own feelings rather than work through and grow in acceptance for his truth as well as her own. She could not fathom the idea that I could possibly be happy with such an "opinionated, misogynic man," overlooking the fact of course that she herself was showing signs of being an extremely opinionated, misandrist woman. I certainly did not have the patience or interest to explain it to her, so that is as far as the conversation went for me. As Patrice took over, I stood quietly beside him as he worked his magic on this couple. This was basically routine, whether we were at a one of his comedy shows, at the mall, or at a restaurant talking to random strangers or at home talking amongst family and friends. Generally, everyone would eventually appreciate and be amazed at the utter existence of truth in our relationship, but they questioned how one could handle such uncensored, explicit candor.

I understand why the idea of hearing the hardcore truth all the time would seem unbearable, and yes, dealing with hardcore truth is difficult, but with truth, you will never be confused about where you stand with the other person. That alone eliminates worry and doubt and will ultimately strengthen your trust and bond with that person. For me, being in a peaceful relationship is what is most important, and I just do not believe you can have peace without truth. I hate lies because I hate confusion, and lies typically result in a lot of wasted time and pain. While the truth may sting, you at least have the opportunity to try and work through whatever it is or decide that it is not something that you are interested in working on with that person. Either way, you have the option of deciding if you are going to stay, because it is within your range of compromise, or move on with the understanding that this person is just not compatible with you, as opposed to living a lie that comes out in the end and crushes you and your ability to move on without carrying heavy emotional baggage into the next relationship.

Cliché as it may sound, as the old saying goes, "The truth shall set you free." Patrice would say that to me a lot whenever I was highly defensive and resistant about something and could not see the light of what he was trying to teach me in the moment. Many times, I would not see what Patrice was trying to convey to me until I saw it being explained or displayed by others. Watching Patrice preach, if you will, never got old. I admired his intelligence and patience and was honored that he believed in me enough to want me to write about his philosophies in a book. Yet, I still did not take the necessary steps towards putting a book into action. But, over time, Patrice kept encouraging me to write, and I finally presented him with an outline of what I thought were the most significant factors that helped me learn best. He not only approved of the outline and found it to be very accurate, he also looked at me and said, *"You're gonna have a best seller.*" He kissed me on my forehead, gave the outline back to me, and walked away.

Unfortunately, Patrice passed long before I was able to bring that initial outline to life in this book. The following chapters do not only represent that general outline he approved many years ago; they also contain, in detail, the foundation of his most dominant philosophies and concepts that enabled us to have a wonderful, loving relationship for ten years. Some of the points you will read are familiar stories and ideas that you may have heard him express publically on the radio, from his regular appearances on Opie and Anthony, to his own relationship show on Sirius XM called "The Black Phillip Show," to his many stand-up comedy specials and live club appearances, and some of them may be new. If you were a close friend and have ever been to our house, then you know that Patrice delivering his soliloquies on stage, on television, or on radio to thousands of people was no different than Patrice delivering those same thoughts and philosophies to a few people sitting on our couch. In this book, I hope to make you feel less like a fan, and more like a family friend in our home.

What you will get out of this book is not only an in depth explanation and interpretation of what Patrice meant by any particular subject or statement he made, you will also get very personal stories where these philosophies were put to the test. Overall, Patrice was a teacher and wanted to share all that he had in him. Again, he had a magical way of taking complex subjects and simplifying them to make perfect sense to the average Joe and Jane. When Patrice and I first met, I was certainly an average thinking Jane, and the only credit I give myself to this day for all that I have learned, and all the knowledge that he placed in me before he passed away, is that I listened and applied. Now it is my responsibility to honor him by sharing with you what he put inside of me by releasing the information as he requested of me many years ago. My only request from you moving forward in

THE NATURAL ORDER

If you are going to live against your own true nature, then how could you ever really be happy? In order to find peace within yourself that will eventually lead to happiness in any type of relationship, you must first take a long hard look in the mirror and accept who you are without judgment. When I first met Patrice, I was an emotionally damaged person. Aside from all of the daddy issues that I had growing up, I also had a few significant romantic relationships with men that shaped my perspective. I viewed both men and women in such a negative way that I was immensely broken. One relationship that I experienced along the way, however, was not damaging at all. This particular affair taught me the benefits of knowing the truth upfront and carried over into my future relationship with Patrice. In fact, all of these prior experiences ultimately set me up to be ready for a man like Patrice, so before I get into how he taught me to love myself as a woman, and him as a man, by initially clarifying the natural order of things, I should first give you a little background on these previous relationships.

My first boyfriend and heartbreak was my high school sweetheart. I was in (what I thought was) a monogamous relationship with him for four years, starting in my sophomore year. Unbeknownst to me, my best friend (whom I was close to since we were in elementary school) was also in a relationship with him for three of those same four years. Yes, to be clear, my best friend was sneaking around with my boyfriend for three years, and I was completely unaware of their relationship the entire time. When I found out, of course, I was crushed. It seemed as if everyone in small-town USA knew about this ongoing affair these two had except me. I felt like a fool, and for obvious reasons, became very distrustful of both men and women in general. I could not imagine what I had possibly done to deserve being hurt so deliberately and deeply, and I was lost without clear guidance or direction. In typical young girl fashion, I wrote my best friend off as an unscrupulous, scheming, jealous, sneaky whore, and ended our friendship for life. I even giggled maliciously when I later discovered he got her pregnant while she was still in college. I found it ironic that her contribution to my heartache and pain resulted in her life goals and dreams being put on hold and eventually diminished. She left school and never amounted to what she originally intended to be when she was young and hopeful. The vengeful side of me thought that she deserved whatever kind of misery was brought upon her for the pain that she caused in my life. I would later learn forgiveness and empathy, but at that particular moment, the devastated young girl in me marveled at her apparent agony with a false sense of redemption. As for the guy, of course, I could not get over him and kept a dysfunctional on-again, off-again, abusive relationship with him for years.

Prior to finding out he was cheating on me, I thought that he was a good boyfriend. I was also very confident that I was a good girlfriend to him, so I thought we had a bright future together. He was a star athlete who worked really hard in three different areas of sports, and he seemed to always be physically hurt. Sometimes during football season, his injuries would be so severe that he could not even sit up in bed on his own. In those instances, I always made myself available to help him do whatever he needed. Even though I lived only five minutes away from where we went to school, I would get up an extra hour early and walk to his house (which was significantly further away) to take him breakfast and help him get dressed. I even did his homework for him more times than I am proud to say. I was only a teenager, but being a loyal, supportive, caring, nurturing female has always been part of my nature, like most women. I had the traditional instincts of a wife and treated our relationship like a marriage, just as I would treat most of my future relationships with men. Considering he paid me back for my loyalty and love by spending all of his fun, healthy time with my best friend,

5

the side chick, I suppose it is fair to say this experience was my first example of what many married women complain about in their lives. Why is it that my loyalty and love only resulted in pain and dishonesty, I wondered? Eventually, I wrapped up all of my tears, bottled up the betrayal inside as resentment, and moved on.

When I was in college, I met the man who would become my daughter's father. Out of respect for my daughter, I will keep most of the details of that relationship private. I will only point out the necessary fact that it was another experience in which I went above and beyond domestically as a woman and received little in return. The same lack of fun and excitement, and the feelings of being taken for granted that I experience in my high school relationship, were definitely present, which of course raised my suspicions of infidelity. Why is it that when you get into a serious, committed relationship with a man, all of the fun goes out of the window and to another woman, I wondered? While there were certainly bigger issues in our relationship than just that, and no infidelities were ever proven, to keep things simple and respectful, let's just say that I moved on. My daughter was only one year old when I broke off the relationship, and I never looked back or regretted leaving. I remember telling him that since our baby was a girl, I could not allow myself to settle in an unhappy relationship for fear that she would someday do the same. To lead my daughter by example, I knew that I had to someday find a truthful, sincere man that would love me completely without taking advantage of my domestic, submissive nature. I decided that until I met that person, it would be best to just be single.

I was so damaged, broken, and frustrated that I succumbed to the idea that the type of man I desired probably did not exist; being in a relationship at that point seemed, quite frankly, stupid. My impression of relationships as a whole was that the side chicks of the world were the ones having all of the fun and reaping the positive benefits of the men; therefore, it would be foolish to keep putting energy into being someone's wife only to be left at home in confusion doing chores. So, with my young, misguided, damaged heart and my confused mentality about men, I began casually dating with the intention of not getting in a serious relationship with anyone. In fact, I preferred to date men who were already in relationships with someone so that I knew for sure that I was on the opposite side of my prior experiences. I also wanted to be sure that he would not have a reason to lie to me about cheating. Right or wrong, that was my mentality at that time. That particular mentality was not only a result of the emotional baggage I carried but also the lack of maturity that I had in my twenties, and to be quite honest, after all of my failed domestic attempts, in my head, it was clearly time to just have a good time. This is when I met a famous comedian that I will refer to throughout this book as, Marlow Key.

I spent about a year or so in a non-committed, casual dating relationship with Marlow, in what proved to be the least damaging experience of them all. Now, I must point out that Marlow was not married during the time I spent with him, but he was definitely in a relationship with a woman he loved. He was honest about his situation from the very beginning, and he made no apologies or excuses. He never spoke about his relationship with many details. I knew she existed in a high position in his life, and that was all I needed to know. He was forthcoming about how much he loved her and I'm sure he felt obligated to her as a man not only because she was the mother of his children but also because she was the one who saved his life when he had a heat stroke that left him helpless and unconscious in the piercing sun. I understood and respected how he felt about her, and it did not affect how I felt towards him, nor did it affect my desire to spend time with him or vice versa. I was simply enjoying my time as his side chick, and he was enjoying having me whenever he arranged for

9

me to be with him wherever he was at the time. Not only did this relationship confirm my thoughts on what happens on the other side of the cheating fence, but it was also my first time seeing firsthand how it was possible for a man to love the woman he is with, even though he is cheating. I realized and knew that the time he was spending with me had absolutely nothing to do with how much he loved his woman. For a young woman with little understanding about men, that was a huge discovery that would help me in my future development with Patrice.

By spending nothing but relaxed, no-pressure time with Marlow, I received exactly what I was looking for in a casual relationship and more. Eventually I grew to realize that being a side chick was just as unfulfilling as being a lonely housewife. While Marlow never treated me badly or made me feel like I was not special to him in my own way, I knew that his affection and time for me would always be limited. I was never in competition in my mind or heart with whom I knew he would eventually marry, so our relationship just ran its course and faded away. He is the only man that I have ever dealt with in my life (including Patrice) that did not leave me with negative baggage to carry over into my next relationship. In fact, my experiences with Marlow helped me to further realize what my true desire for a man was and the type of man I that I should be on the lookout for in my future. I was now clear on what I wanted in a husband. I wanted to be with an intelligent, honest, powerful, dominant man who would hold me in high regard and make me his wife, while maintaining the ability to have fun with me like a mistress so that he would not feel like he needed to cheat or lie. But in my mind I did not know if it was possible to find a man that would be able to appreciate both sides of me as a woman, or if those two sides of me were something that men would always have to keep separate.

Collectively, what I learned from all of these relationships in different ways was that women are constantly confused, hurt, and frustrated by men who lie.

But what I could not figure out was why men felt like

they had to lie to the women they claimed to love? I do

not find it coincidental that the only relationship I was in

which I never felt lied to prior to Patrice was with

Marlow. The beauty of being a side chick (in most cases,

in which the woman is aware of their side-chick status) is

that you get to experience a man in his uncensored, true

form. Men can have fun, be very open, and ultimately

become very close to their mistresses because in most

cases, they are uninhibited and just being themselves,

period. But I knew in my heart that "side chick" was not

the label I ultimately wanted to carry. I knew that I had a

lot to offer as a woman and deserved to be a wife. I am a

loyal, loving, dedicated woman, who is flexible and

compromising, and I have an unbelievable amount of

admiration and adoration for the male species. I had all of

these great qualities and more, yet and still, the best

relationship I had had up to this point was as someone's

side chick. There had to be a way, I thought, to fuse my

domestic, nurturing, dedicated housewife qualities with my side-chick mistress qualities. I did not know if I would ever meet a man who would subscribe to such a concept, but I did know that if such a man existed, the first thing on the list that he would have to be is honest.

"I like hoes." — Patrice O'Neal

In the summer of 2002, by divine alignment, I met probably the most brutally honest man on planet Earth. It was the summer after the World Trade Center attacks, and I had been living in the New York area for several years at this point trying to get my foot in the door as an actress. My roommate at the time referred me to a casting director that she was close friends with, and he provided a rare opportunity for me to work on a Spike Lee movie in order to become SAG eligible. I was so excited and grateful, naïvely thinking that my life as an actress was about to take off. I was booked to work the ADR studio session (a voiceover session in which actors come into a sound studio to fill in the additional sound we hear on screen in the movies in the background). It was only a one-day job, but I finally felt like a legitimate actor and expected this single day of work to change my life forever. Unfortunately, my life as an actor did not change much at all; the course of my life changed dramatically that afternoon however, when I met Patrice.

Patrice played a bouncer in the Spike Lee movie 25th Hour, and he, as well as some of the other main actors, was present at the ADR session. After the session was over, people lingered and talked outside of the studio. A few women, including my roommate, gravitated towards this very large loquacious man. Following behind my very social roommate, I found myself in a cipher that would change my life forever. It was a Tuesday, and Patrice, the center of attention, was inviting all of the women in this cipher to his Friday show at Caroline's on Broadway, where he would be doing stand-up comedy. He directly invited everyone—except me. I did not quite understand why, but I spoke up and said, "Well, why can't I come?" with my best ghetto girl voice and sassy attitude. He blew his breath and said, *"I guess you can come if you come with her* (referring to my roommate) *since I already invited her, and I suppose she was gonna bring you anyway, unfortunately."* I did not understand why I was receiving the cold shoulder from this stranger, since it did not appear as if he knew any of the other females any more than he knew me. So what was the problem? What did I do?

Curiosity, as they say, kills the cat, and I not only went to his show that Friday at Caroline's on Broadway, I also began to hang around him any chance I got thereafter. Time passed, and he eventually explained to me that he did not like me the first day he met me because I had what he considered "pretty girl syndrome." Pretty girl syndrome is basically a sense of entitlement that he felt most woman carried around with them (mostly) subconsciously. Considering his prior experiences with really attractive women, he said that sense of entitlement was usually topped off with unbearable amount of arrogance that left most of them unlikeable and confusingly single. He felt that I had an extreme case of pretty girl syndrome and that he was going to do for me what no other man in my life had ever done before; instead of trying to have sex with me, he would become a real friend and teach me a thing or two about men. He wanted to be my mentor and teach me how to "rise above my vagina and my prettiness." He said that if I wanted people, especially men, to see my value as a woman, then I had to become more valuable than my physicality. I had no clue what he meant by all of this at first. I thought he was insane and presumptuous, considering he did not know me very well. Besides, in my mind, I had all of these wonderful qualities as a woman that he had yet to see. I later found that he did see my value and potential, but he also saw my resentment, bitterness, pain, and lack of direction. Although we eventually became lovers, which contradicted part of his initial intent, he still did exactly what he intended to do with my mind. Over a ten-year period, I kept an open mind and heart while Patrice imbued me with priceless knowledge through the use of brutal honesty and severe patience. He started this training, if you will, by explaining to me the natural order of men and woman and why he felt today's women were at a loss for happiness.

"Vagina is the great equalizer." –Patrice O'Neal

Many women, especially in American culture, have been ingrained with the idea that girls rule the world. However, if you take a look at the simple fact that there are physically more women in the world but men hold most of the positions of power globally, then you will see that it really is quite the opposite. You can even consider a more spiritual approach and find that biblical studies suggest that men were "made in God's image," and women were made from the man's rib, which basically suggests that God himself is a man. Regardless

17

of where you look, or what you believe spiritually, most examples will point in the direction of men being the far superior being. Of course, everything is debatable, but my purpose is not to dig deep into history or biblical studies and debate back and forth about it. My intention is to use simple analogies to help illustrate Patrice's well-thought-out philosophies that are grounded in logic and reasoning.

The biggest gripe with women Patrice had was the lack of respect and appreciation he felt men received for their daily repression of their "manhood" in order to allow females to feel equal. This suppression went against what Patrice believed to be the natural order of gender roles. Only humans fight against their true nature, Patrice would suggest, and if you break down human beings to their most basic, natural, animalistic instincts, you will see the natural order more clearly. Patrice loved using female cops as an example to illustrate the suppression of manhood. He would approach this idea by first pointing out that in order for a woman to be a cop, men have to "let her" be a cop. Meaning, without her gun, special training, or badge of authority, it would not be likely that she could physically take most men down, whereas men in or out of uniform have somewhat of a more equal chance. *"A female cop cannot arrest me without my cooperation or backup,"* Patrice stated, pointing out that in most situations in life, men have to comply and repress their natural "cave man" instincts in order to allow women to dominate them. This creates a false sense of equality that lends itself to a lack of respect for men. It was very typical of many women who heard this to try and debate it with Patrice. They would sometimes do so by redirecting his theory to sports, which I found very interesting, since most of these women had a limited knowledge of sports. However, they would start by making what seemed like a good point at first: these women would suggest to Patrice that with all of his male dominance and strength, he still could never beat someone like Candice Parker one on one in a basketball game. This was their attempt to say that yes, woman can do whatever men can do, and sometimes better. Patrice's minimal retort would prove otherwise, leaving them with no other choice but to agree with him or lash out at him in frustration. *"Probably not,"* he would respond, *"because I am not a professional basketball player. But no woman could beat any man of her equivalent status in whatever it is she does."* Simply put, Candice Parker could never beat Lebron James.

Whether it was one on one or while performing on stage, Patrice loved to spark the attention of his audience by posing questions and allowing for a retort. One question that would get an uproarious response was, *"Ladies, if you lost your pussy in an accident, how would you keep your man?"* Women would shout out different answers from the front to the back of the venue such as, "Suck his dick" and "Let him fuck me in my ass." Allowing time for the possibility of different answers to emerge, Patrice would give the women in the audience ample time to speak their minds. Then, once he felt he had allotted enough time and found that there were no new or unique answers emerging, he would squash their enthusiasm and quiet the entire crowd with one observant statement: *"See ladies, I gave you a chance, and no one said, 'Learn how to play Xbox,' 'Learn how to watch sports intelligently,' or learn anything that your man likes to do. You just qualified yourself as a series of holes, but you want us (men) to treat you special."*

Patrice was in love with the opposite sex, and he was obsessed with trying to discover new ways to help women think outside of their "box"—literally. His ultimate mission was simply to give women different options on how to think so that we can live in harmony with men as opposed to against them. He wanted to get women to fully understand and accept their natural roles as a woman, then build from there. To help aid in his attempt, one of the analogies he used was "men are hunters and women are the hunted." For a hunter to be able to eat, he has to be trained. He has to learn many

21

things, such as how to use a gun, and he has to learn all about his prey: where to find it, the best strategies to take it down, and so on and so forth. The prey, on the other hand, does not need to know anything about the hunter in order to be captured and consumed. The prey basically just has to appear juicy and delicious. In parallel to relationships, Patrice compared how men trained socially as young boys to learn how to "get" girls by observation and development of charm and wit, while women at a young age were mostly developing their beauty skills. So it is no wonder that we find many beautiful women with very little personality to offer. However, you may find that women who are less attractive tend to be more down to Earth, or easy going, because they innately know that they have to do additional things in order to make themselves more attractive to the hunter. Either way, generally speaking, the hunter is technically the one who is in control of the dynamic. It is only when the prey picks up the gun and starts shooting at the hunter when things go awry.

"Women win on the front end; men win on the backend." —Patrice O'Neal

In an effort to remind a man who relinquished his authority and gave his "gun" away to a woman in order to "get" her vagina that he is the hunter and he is in control, Patrice would say to him, *"You're better than her."* Continuing, he would ask, *"What is she bringing to the table other than her vagina that is better than what you are bringing to the table as a man?"* All of these statements may seem a bit harsh, but it's hard to argue his logic behind it; and that is, realistically, a man can typically find another woman much easier than she can find another man. When someone hears this, red flags of disagreement are immediately raised. Patrice, however, was always prepared with undeniable, common sense logic to back up all of his statements. Anyone who looks at this particular theory— that a man can get a woman easier than a woman can get a man—on the surface would quickly say that the

23

statement is foolish, considering that men are the hunters and in most cases will do whatever it takes to get their prey. Patrice would agree that yes, she can get *dick* easier than he can get *pussy*; however, she will never be able to find a man willing to be locked down with her and put up with all of her crap in a committed relationship as quickly as he can find a woman to be committed to him in a relationship. In most cases this is absolutely true. Most men want sex right away, while most women want commitment.

"Men want pussy without giving up time. Women want time without giving up pussy." –Patrice O'Neal

If we find a man that actually has the desire to be in a relationship with us and spend time with us outside of his sexual interests, shouldn't we be obliged to recognize the value in that and show some appreciation? We certainly expect men to show appreciation and gratitude for our vaginas, don't we? Sometimes we are so

24

busy protecting our surface value that we don't realize all we have to do to increase our worth instantaneously is to remove the thick wall of false dominance we have built up over the years that we think aids us in our demand for what is actually the wrong type of respect. Far too often women want to be treated like a lady but seek to be respected as a man. That's a ridiculous thought. A man's presence alone demands a certain level of respect that a woman could never acquire. That is not to say that a woman's presence doesn't demand respect at all, but a woman's presence is different; therefore, a different type of respect is acquired. There is absolutely nothing wrong with what you are and what you get as a result. You should always *and only* want to be respected as what you are, and if you are a woman, embrace the respect that comes with that instead of being resentful of what a man is and trying to take what he has, thereby remaining attractive, desirable, and, most importantly, valuable.

In general, Patrice spoke in terms of roles and value. Knowing your role and your value as a woman in a relationship is very important, but that does not mean you have to go against what you like or dislike based on culture or society. In the most successful relationships, you will find that the two people complement each other without marginalizing one another or making the other person feel as if it is their "duty" to do anything in particular. Everything is based off of desire to increase the happiness of the other person, and that is the type of relationship I had with Patrice. We did not subscribe to any set of written or unwritten rules. We wrote our own set of rules that complimented the other's abilities and desires. For instance, Patrice loved to cook. We did not fight against his desire to cook based on the fact that in many cultures, traditionally, cooking is the woman's job. My approach with this, as with everything, was to show appreciation and support for his desire by finding a way to help make what it is he was doing easier. In the case of him cooking, I would make it easier for him by cleaning

26

up after him as he went along and assisting him with whatever he asked me to do. I would also try and clean up after our meal as well, but Patrice would usually make that part of the occasion collaborative. We, without verbally setting any type of rules, developed a system that worked for the both of us, which is how you can best show love and respect for your partner.

I believe that as a woman, our only job as a wife is to make it extremely easy for a man to be a good husband. That is it. It sounds very simple, but I know it is easier said than done. However, there is nothing wrong with developing an understanding mindset and living in such a way that you excel within your relationship as you are by recognizing not only your strengths, but also your weakness without bringing your man down in areas in which he is better. It is ok to admit that men are naturally stronger than us and that we look at them as our protectors and providers, just as it is ok to admit that women tend to be more nurturing and better caregivers than most men. You do not see men complaining that they can't breastfeed babies, so why do we force ourselves to act as if we don't need them for certain things when we really do? Yes, we can do many things ourselves without the assistance of a man, but we are not talking about ability per say, we are talking about happiness. Yes, I can take the garbage out at night to the dumpster in the dark corner, but yes, I am certainly more vulnerable to attack than a man. Quite frankly, I would rather he take the risk. Conversely, it is also ok to recognize and adjust when the other's interests cross over into the other's innate abilities, as in the case with Patrice cooking. What is not ok is to for you or your man to do anything just because you think that is what should be done based on rules set outside of your bond. Get to know your mate and respect his or her strengths and weaknesses. Also keep in mind that the more you try to unnaturally live in a man's shoes, as a woman, it only makes you appear weaker, not stronger.

Bottom line ladies, you will never be a man, and that is ok. You can, however, get to know the species that he is, much like he got to know us in elementary and high school while we were busy beautifying ourselves and building habits of entitlement. In finding a way to live in harmony with men, however, we can only attempt to learn to speak his language. Approach this concept the same way you would approach learning any new language, considering the fact that learning to speak his language does not make you a man. If you learned to speak Mandarin, for instance, that would not make you Asian. It only makes you a better communicator with Mandarin-speaking Asian people and other people who speak the language. Additionally, if you were going to learn a language such as Mandarin, you would not only have to learn the words to become fluent; you would have to take the time to study the culture, engage with those who speak the language, be attentive to details in effort to pick up on the proper accents, and make many new discoveries that would take you beyond your

29

comfort zone. And even with all of these efforts, once you became fluent, people would still be able to tell that Mandarin is not your first language, especially the native speakers of that language. However, the time and effort that you put into trying to communicate in Mandarin as best as possible would likely be recognized, appreciated, and respected. Likely, men do not ever expect us to think exactly as they do. All they really want is for us to respect them for the man that they are (without challenging their place or trying to change them) so that they can treat us like a good woman should be treated in their minds. After all, most men just want to position themselves as a king so that he can upgrade his woman to the highest position in the land of his life as his queen. He wants to treat you royally and shower you with all the benefits that come with being his queen, but you have to let him be the king he is in order to do whatever it is he can do to elevate you in his life. If we just take the time to understand the animal that has taken many years to understand us, maybe we can get along better.

Patrice and I respected one another, and that is what kept us together. As I mentioned earlier, I only credit myself with one thing in making our relationship successful, and that is that I was willing to listen and do my best to understand him and his desires as a man and not marginalize or try to change them. In other words, I wanted to learn his language. I only wanted to know how to work with him just as equally as he was working with me. Respect and love to me are the same thing. You cannot convince me that you have one for me without the other. You have to respect your man in his natural masculine position. Do not dare to expect to get respect and love from a man without being willing to give both in return. That is what real equality is ladies. Not some forced, unrealistic reality of false truth. As it stands now, overall, male/female equality is out of balance because men let us think we are equal by submitting, just to avoid annoying arguments, while women unfairly and disrespectfully ignore their struggles and desires as men.

31

The best thing you can do to have a successful relationship is to know the animal that you are, know the animal that you are dealing with, make an attempt to learn its language, and check your ego at the door. You are not entitled to anything that he has to offer.

*C*hapter 2

*E*ntitlement

"Equate how you feel about your vagina to how we feel about our time and our space."

—   *Patrice O'Neal*

ENTITLEMENT

For the first year or so of my relationship with Patrice, whenever I would visit him at his apartment, there were a few things I was sure to see: his roommate, a good plate of food, and a picture of his ex-girlfriend on the mirror in his bedroom. Before Patrice and I met, he spent some time honing his comedic skills in London. While staying in London, he not only got his comedy style and rhythm together, but that is also where he met his second long-term girlfriend. He described her as a tall, voluptuous woman with a kind heart and pretty face. He always spoke very highly of her and said that we were a lot alike. When I asked how, he said, *"I attract crazy bitches,"* suggesting that the two of us had very similar issues as women that he felt obligated to try and help fix. He also said that if we ever met, we would probably get along really well, that is, if we could get past our "girl shit." That "girl shit" he was referring to was territorial jealousy and entitlement.

34

I must admit, I felt naturally territorial every time I looked at her picture on his mirror. My inner dialogue would question why I should I have to look at his ex-girlfriend every time I came over to visit. That inner dialogue grew especially intense once Patrice and I became intimate. However, Patrice was not interested in having me get my way with him emotionally without good reason and expressed communication beyond feelings. His mission to get me (and every other woman he came across) to think outside of the box stayed consistent the entire time I knew him. He said that he felt it was a man's responsibility to give women "different options on how to think" and felt that it was a disservice to women whenever a man would just submit to a woman's demands and not make her work diligently at justifying why she felt any particular way. He forced me to think outside of my own comfort zone by challenging me as to why I felt that he should take the picture down. He would not accept any answers from me that had anything to do with insecurity or jealousy, and urged rational thinking. *"Tell me why I should take it down with a good reason that is disconnected from your emotions and the entitlement you feel in that you think I should take it down 'just because,' and I might take it down,"* he said. Of course, I could not find any reason for him to take it down that was not linked to my emotions or entitlement, so the picture remained. I cannot put a time frame on how long, but I can say that it was there for so long that I just became used to it and it no longer affected me when I saw it on the mirror. In fact, I became so used to it that its presence, in some ways, became invisible to my eyes. As my relationship with Patrice grew, my confidence in our relationship grew past whatever insecurities I had about the picture and the picture itself became irrelevant. I remember when he finally took the picture down, he said that he grew to a point where he not only felt that I had earned his respect enough to take down the picture, but he also started to feel bad about the picture being on the mirror. For me, that was a triumphant moment. That experience helped me to realize how to be strong and surpass surface insecurities by helping me to understand

and accept that just because a person is with you in a new

relationship does not mean that they are no longer

human and have to disregard their memories or emotions

for others in their past. The picture had meaning to

Patrice. He loved her, but it just did not work out, much

like his time spent in London. He found a better life back

home in America. But that did not mean that he had to

erase all the love and memories from that particular

moment of time in his life. I learned that his old life was

no threat to his new life, which I was now a huge part of

in this new time and space. It wasn't until I lived through

that experience that I saw how strong him not taking that

picture down made me as a woman and how secure it

made me in our relationship.

From Patrice's point of view, in the beginning of

our arguments about whether or not he should take the

photo down, he said to me that it would be best if he

took it down when he was ready to, not when I told him

to. He said that he could not release a certain amount of power over him to me that I had not earned. He also felt I was not trained to handle that kind of power. Patrice had learned from his past experiences how power corrupts people, especially in relationships and especially with women, and should he let me rule him with my emotional demands, our relationship would have been doomed from that point forth. He was saving our relationship from the very beginning by not letting me control him. His logic was that if I made him take that picture down, it wouldn't be long before I made other demands, which ultimately would lead to me controlling him and him resenting me. So, to initially help me understand his logic about taking the picture down before he was ready to take it down, he used his bully theory. *"If you let a bully take your lunch money on Monday because you are afraid to lose a fight, then he will be back to take your lunch money on Tuesday, Wednesday, Thursday, and Friday. He won't just go away and say "Thank you." In fact, he will be drunk off of the power more than the money he is getting from you, and until you are willing to "take an L"* [loss] *and stand up for yourself, win lose or draw, you will continue to be controlled."* This was one of Patrice's earliest examples of entitlement in our relationship, and it was applied throughout our relationship for the rest of our days together. He always told me that he was with me out of desire, not obligation, and that if I put the fire out on the desire, then he could still love me from afar, but he would no longer be in a relationship with me, just as in the case with his ex-girlfriend from London. There were two things that broke them up, according to him, and he made it a point to tell me these things so that I would not make the same mistakes.

The major problem was her co-dependency on him, which he discovered when he returned to the United States from London after being offered his first stand-up comedy television special on Showtime. He said that if it was not for the Showtime offer, he was going to move to London permanently because he thought that was where his career was going to flourish. He loved the freedom in comedy overseas. He felt that the audiences there were not in a rush to laugh, which allowed for him to paint a picture with his set. The audiences in London were open to the process of his storytelling delivery and slower pace, which rewarded them with a large payoff of laughter in the end of a story as opposed to the fast-paced, punch line after punch line demands of the audiences in the United States. Once he returned to the States, he invited his girlfriend to come stay with him to see how it would go. He said that she became very codependent and grew weaker the longer she stayed. She would not even go outside without him, which made him feel that she was too weak to be in a relationship with him, especially if she would have to move to the United States.

However, the biggest lesson about entitlement and respect that I learned through his stories about her stay with him was his "respect trickles down" theory. One day he said he was hanging out in the living room, talking with his friends and roommate, and she began to make her presence known by stomping her way past them, walking back and forth from the bedroom, past the living room where they were sitting, and into the kitchen, then back to the bedroom with a nasty attitude and heavy aura of bad energy. He identified this behavior as a quiet, subtle protest that she did not want him to have company. Not only was she uncomfortable leaving the house without him, she also wanted him all to herself whenever they were home. She did not verbally say she did not want him to have company or that she would rather he spend all his time in the room alone with her, but her actions helped Patrice conclude his thinking that such was the case. After her aggressive pacing happened a few times, he pulled her to the side and took her to the bedroom to explain to her the respect trickles down theory. He accused her of being rude and childish and explained to her that the only reason the guys in the other room were not calling her the "ignorant bitch" that she was being was because they respected him, not her. She was receiving undeserved respect through his relationship with his friends because the respect they had for him trickled down to her. He continued explaining that she was putting him in a bad position to unnecessarily defend her and that he was not going to do that on her behalf since she was acting out of order. Her actions showed a lack of respect for him as a man. For most men, these situations are very embarrassing, and it also makes the woman look very childish. So, instead of defending her erratic behavior to his friends, Patrice had excused himself from his friends to put his woman in check. I do not know what her response was to Patrice after he confronted her about her behavior. I was only given the details of that situation from his point of view as an example of how not to be when it comes to entitlement, respect, space, and time.

Patrice had learned in his prior relationship with his high school sweetheart not to ever prolong the inevitable. He felt that he had stayed in the relationship with his high school girlfriend far past the point of his desire primarily for the fear of hurting her feelings. Sacrificing his happiness for the sake of hers left him very frustrated and resentful, and he vowed to himself that he would never do that again. Once you have identified in a relationship that it will not work, especially after trying, you should not linger. It only causes increased pain for both people. It is ok to discover that, although you care for someone, you and that person may not be a match. So, without prolonging the inevitable in his current situation, he eventually sent his then girlfriend back to London, and the only thing left of her in his life was the picture on the mirror and a pair of boots in the closet. Some people may remember a bit Patrice did about me finding her boots in the closet and him refusing to throw them away just to appease my childish jealousy. If so, and you are wondering if those are the boots in this story, then yes, to answer your thought bubble, those are the same boots, and much like the picture on the mirror, he got rid of the boots in his own time and on his own terms, not mine.

Again, I was so used to seeing the picture every time I came over, and after getting to know Patrice and his purpose for keeping the picture up (as well as the boots in the closet), it bothered me less and less, to the point of irrelevancy. The day I noticed that the picture was finally gone, he told me that it had been gone for a few days already and that he was proud of me that I did not even notice. He felt that I had showed so much growth, improvement, and endurance that I deserved a "promotion." He said that I endured that situation long enough and earned the right to not have to look at her every time I came over to spend time with him. He took the picture down because he wanted to, not because I made him. I felt proud. I felt so clear about what entitlement was at this point. I also understood better what freedom as an individual within a relationship meant to Patrice, especially when he told me about how he started to feel bad about the picture being on the mirror and then taking it down on his own terms. He said that once he started to feel independently bad about the picture being on the mirror is when he knew it was time to take it down. I had earned a level of respect from him that was not only undeniable, but he was happy to give it to me, as opposed to being forced to give it to me despite his point of view. I also developed an understanding of, and empathy for Patrice as a person. Just because a person moves on from a relationship, it does not mean that person has to ignore or despise the people of their past in order to make the new person in their life feel secure. After going through this experience and learning about their relationship and why it did not last, whatever insecurities I had in the beginning slowly and naturally faded away. In addition, I must emphasize that I felt better knowing that something I once felt entitled to (him taking the picture down), I had earned. It took time, but it instilled so much strength in me, which helped me to deal with jealously and insecurity in a new way, not only with that situation, but in future situations as well.

Patrice's philosophy on entitlement basically boils down to possession and freedom. In fact, most of Patrice's philosophies can be boiled down to the basic concept of freedom. He was always fighting for freedom in everything he spoke about, from domestic relationships to freedom of speech in politics and religion. Freedom was the most important factor in his life, and I would argue the point that it is the most important factor in most of our lives, both men and women, but from different points of view. With that being said ladies, do not underestimate how much more a man's freedom means to him than it does to us in relationships. As a woman, with our loving, nurturing emotions in the forefront, we are usually very flexible in compromising our freedoms in relationships. In fact, if you are like me, you might enjoy a man who makes his requests known to do or not do certain things. However, with men, their freedom comes first above everything. You have to understand that just because you are in a relationship with someone does not mean you or your partner are no longer individual people. We have to respect that men must maintain a sense of freedom, and they especially want to keep their manhood intact. Just because you are in a committed relationship with a man does not mean that he wants you to turn into his nagging momma and give him a curfew. You are both still individual people. You are what Patrice would call "separate but together."

"Men want to be alone, but we don't want to be by ourselves." —Patrice O'Neal

When Patrice took me to Brazil for my birthday for fourteen days in 2006, we enjoyed our time there in separate rooms. We both agreed that it was not necessary to always be up under each other, bumping into each other getting dressed, sharing closet space, and living

47

every waking minute with each other just because we were on vacation. In fact, that is how we lived our regular life at home. With possible different sleep patterns and habits, why do couples find it better to constantly argue over little things like space when (if you can afford to do so) you should just live with more individual space. It is ok to be separate but together. We slept in the same bed on vacation just like at home, but it was not mandatory if we were not ready to sleep at the same time. Whether at home or away, Patrice and I were rarely ready to go to sleep at the same time, but eventually we found ourselves in bed together at some point in the night. I would usually fall asleep before him but had a habit of sleeping very lightly, so I could hear how many times he went to the bathroom at night. If I did not feel or hear him get out of the bed to pee, I would wake him to make sure he was ok and that he was not holding it. When you love someone who is burdened with multiple diseases like high blood pressure and diabetes, it becomes your disease as well. For years, I made sure that I would check him sporadically through the night once he fell asleep to make sure he was breathing. If he was up and I wanted to sleep, or vice versa, we always had our own rooms we could retreat to, but I always made sure that we ended up in the same bed when he was ready to sleep. We both enjoyed our space, although I admittedly was up under him one hundred times more than he would be under me, and I learned to not take his distance personally. Men in some ways view our neediness for attention and our desires to cuddle in a similar way as us mothers might view our children's demands for attention and affection. Of course we love our children and want to give them all the love and affection in the world, but sometimes (lots of times) we just need some time alone. It is not a reflection of how much we love or do not love our children if we want them to leave us alone to watch our favorite show, or while we cook, or while we read, or whatever it is we are doing. Sometimes we enjoy doing those same things with our children, but it is ok as a human being to want to be left alone sometimes. We have to look at a man's alone time away from us in the same respect and understand that everything will be ok—if not better.

When Patrice was teaching me his theory on men wanting to be alone, but not by themselves, he went back to the idea of entitlement and possessiveness. Eventually, if you leave him alone long enough, he will find you and want to accommodate your needs to be heard, held or whatever it is you desire. But just like in the case of the picture of his ex on the mirror, you are not entitled to his time and space and have to respectfully wait for it. You have to inspire the desire in him to accommodate your needs, not force it. People sometimes think if they deny the idea that they need their space, that's love: forcing themselves to deny their basic human need. That is not love. Love is being empathic to and understanding of your mate. Love is respect for your mate as a person, not a possession. Love is allowing for space without combativeness, a nasty attitude, or unnecessary assumptions. You only build resentment denying yourself or your mate their basic needs, so why would you want to do that? Why build resentment so that even the minimum amount of time spent together is miserable, as opposed to allowing for space and missing each other so that you can enjoy each other when your desire to occupy each other's time and space coincides? With time and understanding of what the other's needs are, eventually, the respect and love you have for one another will help mesh the flow of shared time and space into a perfect rhythm.

As women, we will always be challenged with how to think above our emotions and in a rational, logical state of mind. Men are naturally very practical, so for the most part, even with the most emotional men of them all, they tend to know how to think in terms of practicality and reason first. Patrice taught me not only that I should rise above my emotions, he also taught me how to do it. It is much easier said than done, especially once a month during my menstrual cycle, but the secret to success in this area is quite simple. The secret is having empathy for your man's point of view and acceptance that your first knee jerk reaction to any given situation might just be wrong because you have not thought it through rationally. You cannot just react based on how a situation makes you *feel*. You must first admit that your first thought may just be pure, raw emotion, and if so, it is valid, but it does not make you right or entitled to any particular results. You have to consider his point of view. Every man is not always wrong, and every man is not always lying. A night out with the fellas should not be a threat to you, just as a night out with the girls should not be for him. It is not your job to ruin your man's good time just because he does not want you to tag along, and it does not mean that he is cheating or planning to cheat. It simply means he wants some time out with the fellas, similar to when you just genuinely want to have girl's night out with your friends. Keep in mind with every situation that occurs that may trigger an emotion in you, potentially starting an argument with your man, to take a deep breath and reverse the situation in your mind. Ask yourself, honestly, how you would feel if the shoe were on the other foot. You most likely will come up with a different answer than your emotions are allowing if you think it through. Can you imagine if every time you wanted to hang out with your girls your man insisted on going as well, and if you said no, he had an attitude and did everything imaginable to ruin your night out, like calling your phone every half hour to check on you? I guarantee you ladies, feeling like you have a right to make your man miserable for any reason does not work, and you know that you would not want to be with him if he was doing that to you. So apply the same principles and rules of restraint to yourself that you want him to have for you because double standards will get you nowhere fast.

Chapter 3

Double Standards

"Man honesty becomes misogyny for some reason."

— Patrice O'Neal

DOUBLE STANDARDS

To combat a woman's arrogance and get her to understand her contribution to any particular double standard, you must reverse every situation and match the audacity in which she is saying what she is saying, or doing what she is doing. This was the technique Patrice used, not only with me in our personal relationship, but he used it in life in general. The infamous "You're raping my time" bit from Patrice's Def Comedy Jam appearance is a perfect example. It is also a classic example of how Patrice would set his listeners up before spilling the truth in their ears. For instance, he set up telling women how they are rapists in their own way by saying, *"Here's how to make your man like you and desire what you want, which is love. Equate how you feel about your vagina to how we feel about our time and our space…. I can't fuck you against your will; you gotta desire to want to fuck me. If I fuck you against your will, that's rape. Now if I am on the phone and I say, "Look I got to go," and you say, "Why you gotta go? I want to talk to you some more." You are raping my time. You are taking something from me. No means no, bitch. I said I got to go. Why are you forcing me to stay*

on the phone and talk to you about nothing?"

It is not possible to be the same and to be
different at the same time. So the very fact that men and
women are physically and mentally made up differently
suggests lack of equality. Yes, Patrice believed that a man
and a woman doing the exact same job in society should
be paid the same, but he never wanted to get bogged
down with details and semantics of any argument.
Patrice's interest was to get people to understand and
debate the context of a situation, not the specific little
details that can get you off track and miss the overall
point. His argument on equality ran much deeper than
the surface details, and his fight certainly was not to
marginalize women and their efforts and rights to pursue
their individual happiness. His fight was for the respect
he felt men did not get when considering their differences
in makeup, while women, with little effort or
consideration in many situations will get excused based

on their feminine makeup. That dynamic within itself is not representative of equality. It is clearly taking advantage of double standards. Patrice used to always say the way most people think is *"Good enough is good, if it's good enough for me."* In other words, a person with that mentality feels that if they do something that they feel is ok, then it's ok, but if someone else does something that they feel is wrong, then they, with a judgmental mindset, will consider the other person wrong. But where is the consideration for the feelings of the other person in that particular situation? For instance, Patrice once asked, *"Why is being gay a choice, but tying a bitch up and peeing on her a fetish?"* He made his point vulgar on purpose, considering that there was once a time when homosexual acts were considered just as vulgar and unheard of, but in today's world it is now more acceptable and almost vulgar to consider being gay a bad thing. This drives Patrice's point home a bit, as if to say, technically, both sexual acts are ok if they are ok for the individual participants. Who are you to say it is right or wrong for any reason? What's ironic is that it is very likely that a couple that happens to be into one of the examples, but not the other, is likely to judge the other one as wrong.

In relation to arguments and debates, Patrice said he hated living in a world where, seemingly, no matter what a man does it is wrong and no matter what a woman does it is right. In a sense, Patrice was fighting for male equality. Patrice was considered by many a misogynist because he felt this way and spoke on it fearlessly and relentlessly both in private and in public. Why does a man's truth get marginalized? If a man is honest and says he is not ready for children and wants a woman to get an abortion, that man is demonized and viewed as irresponsible and immature. However, if the woman in that same situation says that she is not ready for children and wants to get an abortion, she is pro-choice and mature in deciding what is best for her life.

Patrice was viewed as a woman hater; however, he was really quite the opposite. He was on a mission to help all people (especially women) find happiness by living in their truth while being accepting of others and their truth. He said that he felt "sorry for the emotional, irrational, entitled beings" that we are, and admittedly considered that very thought alone condescending, yet true. Specifically, he said, *This is so condescending, but the shit I say about women is based on how bad I feel for what they are. It's a sad creature.* He innately knew that our genetic makeup as women left many of us (if not all) lost, in a sense, with our demands and desires and a prisoner to our inherent entitlement. He felt that having the power that comes with a vagina ruined the possibility of natural objective thinking, and that is why women needed to be taught how to think logically above that power. Patrice learned all about double standards at a young age growing up in Boston, Massachusetts, and he felt that he was just the right man to teach this higher level of thinking to both men and women. However, Patrice's very first experience that helped him to develop this higher level of thinking and his philosophy on double standards and more was not with a woman.

When Patrice was ten years old, he was thrown out of summer camp because he chased a little white boy for calling him a nigger. Patrice said that after the little white boy called him a nigger, he ran from Patrice, continuing to tease him, until he reached the area where the camp counselors were standing. Patrice was reprimanded for chasing the little boy and threatening to bring him physical harm. When Patrice gave his reason for chasing him, the little boy denied it, and since there was no proof or evidence of anything but the chase, Patrice was sent home as the villain. At this point, Patrice realized that he must combat racism mentally, not physically. People can set you up to fail, and you can't ever allow something that anyone says spark enough emotion in you that your reaction hurts you more than it hurts the opposition. While that was a lesson in race, it was surely carried over into how he dealt with all people, including women.

Once, I was bartending and came home with a long story about how some guy at work pissed me off. I was so angry that I said I wished I had thrown a beer at this guy's head. Now, I do not remember the details of what happened to anger me that day, but I do remember Patrice's response to my anger. He said, *"Let me tell you something. Your anger and emotion towards this guy is disrespectful to me. Love and hate is the same thing, and if he can spark this much emotion in you whether it is positive or negative, then he can fuck you. So I suggest you handle your emotions differently, unless you are interested in hooking up with this guy."*

Wow, I thought to myself. I certainly was not expecting that, and I definitely was not interested in hooking up with this guy at all. At this point in my relationship with Patrice, I knew his statement was not frivolous. It was definitely something to think about. As I thought about it more and more, I realized that Patrice was right. Many times people do not care what type of attention they get from you. Good or bad, it is still attention, and eventually, if a man is in hunt mode, as long as you are engaging in any type of banter with him, in his mind, he has a chance. So from that point forth, I never let anyone, man or woman, spark enough emotion in me to the point where I would lose my cool. I almost became numb to any harsh words or negative energy that came my way. After all, these people did not matter to me, and the people in my life that did matter to me could possibly be affected by my outrage at someone who doesn't matter. I always kept that in mind moving forward, especially around men. I never wanted my man to think for a second that any other man could get to me emotionally, especially with Patrice as my trainer—my sensei. He was the best at the mental game and I, as his woman and student, was a reflection of him. This made me so much stronger in how I deal with people in general.

The summer camp incident was not the only covert racist experience that Patrice had growing up in Boston that impacted his life. When Patrice was seventeen, he was charged with statutory rape after he and a couple of his friends hooked up and ran a "consensual train" on a fifteen-year-old girl and her friend. The fifteen-year-old girl was Caucasian, and when rumors spread around school about the porn-style frenzy that she had with Patrice and his friends, she eventually cried rape. Due to the fact that she was fifteen, and Patrice was seventeen, he was charged with statutory rape and he had to serve two months of his high school summer break in jail. While he only got sentenced to two months in jail and one-year probation, he still had a rape charge on his record for the rest of his life.

This rape charge hit Patrice hard when, although he had been to Canada many times in the past, he was stopped at the borders and denied entry after driving many hours to go to the Just For Laughs Comedy Festival in Montreal. This was a huge turning point in Patrice's life because it was a moment that sent him on a long drive back home in which he realized that he had no one to call and talk to that could help mentor him through the situation. He, at 40 years old, deeply realized that he never had a father, a father figure, or a mentor in his life. He was the backbone to everyone he knew and realized the importance of why people need someone like him. But whom could he turn to? On this very long ride home, he decided to call his mother. While I did not see it, he told me that he actually cried when he was on the phone with her. He said that his mother could only do what mothers could do, and that is give kind, nurturing words of encouragement. He also said that he knew if he called me, I would say similar things that his mother said, but since I was his wife, he did not want me to see him as weak and in a vulnerable state. For that reason, Patrice ultimately chose to talk to me about it in retrospect as opposed to in the moment. Either way, he knew that he would have to make sense of things on his own and move on from this situation as he did his entire life.

Patrice would never allow himself to feel like a victim, so in order to deal with this particular situation, he thought back to when he was a young man and looked at the rape charges in a totally different light. He came up with a few reasons to feel positive and empathetic about the situation. His first thought was that maybe if he was a young fifteen-year-old white girl in the same situation, it's quite possible he would have done the same thing. Secondly, he knew that the judge was very lenient on the sentencing. He could have served ten years in jail but was only served sixty days with a one-year probation. He pondered to himself that maybe this was God's way of balancing things out. Not necessarily speaking in terms of their individual case, but in context of men and women overall, he pondered the idea that if women had to live with the threat of being raped, then men had to live with the threat of being falsely accused of rape. So in a sense,

Patrice believed that he, as a man, was raped. In the same way that a woman who has actually been raped would have to carry the mental and physical burden of being raped for the rest of her life, he now had to carry the burden of a man who was falsely accused of rape. That particular charge not only gave him insight, but it also helped him to empathize with women in a certain way. His ability to flip every situation and to put things into perspective naturally was impeccable. These experiences carried throughout Patrice's life (and mine); he would never allow me to victimize myself in any story I told. He helped me to always take responsibility for everything I did in any particular situation, even if the other person was wrong. The best example of this is the day I threw pasta out of our car window at a couple of large, arrogant women who would not move out of the street so we could drive by.

Now, let me preface this story: I should be too ashamed to tell it, but the truth is, sometimes the ghetto

66

just jumps out of me when least expected. Growing up, I was the youngest in a click of about ten badass projects girls who could all fight. So of course, I had a lot of mouth. After all, no one was going to let anything happen to the baby of the group. If you had a problem with me, then you had to deal with my crew. You had to get through all of them first before you could lay a hand on me, so I had a lot of attitude, but very few fights under my belt. With this mentality, there I was, years later, with Patrice and my daughter on our way home from dinner at an Italian restaurant in a strip mall area. Patrice was driving his very large Yukon Denali, but he could only drive a little above one mile per hour because there were two very large women in the middle of the street. They were very casually walking and disregarding us driving behind them. They were chatting it up and looking back occasionally as if to say, "Whatever, we will move when we want to move." Now, inside the vehicle, my daughter was in the back seat, oblivious of the entire situation because she was rather young at the time. Patrice was in the driver's seat but not saying a word. I was not speaking on it either, but I was silently becoming furious. In my head, I was thinking about the nerve these women had to just disregard this huge truck behind them and not move out of the way. I became increasingly angry, and I looked over at Patrice to see that his face was very calm and nonchalant. He just shrugged his shoulders as if to say hey, that's what y'all entitled bitches do. Finally, the women, very slowly, started moving towards the sidewalk while continuing their conversation. As the road became clear, Patrice started to drive past them, and I decided to throw my left over pasta at them out of the window. The truck got about 10 feet ahead of them and Patrice stopped the car. I rolled the window up and looked at him, shocked. He rolled my window back down and locked it so that I could not roll it back up. My daughter looked up at me, scared, and said, "Mommy, what's going on?" I could see the two very large women angrily approaching my side of the vehicle through the passenger side mirror. I asked Patrice what he was doing, and he said, *"You're so bad* (meaning tough), *handle your business."* I was so nervous. My mind was racing. I had no clue how to get out of this unexpected situation. As they approached my window, screaming at me, I turned to them and said, "My bad. I apologize. I shouldn't have done that. I lost my patience and my cool. My period must be coming." Of course, I cannot tell you exactly what their response was because I was terrified, and they were yelling at me, but after I apologized to them, Patrice raised the window and drove off. For about sixty seconds, there was dead silence in the truck. I knew I was wrong, and I knew Patrice was about to let me have it. Patrice began to speak and he said, *"You should be ashamed of yourself, to do something so low class like throw pasta out the window—and in front of your daughter. First of all, you're with me. Did you see me get angry? No. Did you see me even beep the horn at them? No. So why did you take it upon yourself to do something you can't get yourself out of?"* I was completely silent, not answering any of his questions because I knew that they were all rhetorical. I knew he would eventually clear up his point in a way that I could understand. He continued: *"I will tell you why. Because you are with me, so you're bad* (tough). *You wouldn't have done that shit if I wasn't with you. You would have composed yourself and your impatient anger. But because you're with me, you got the nerve to throw pasta out the window, assuming that I am going to protect you. So if you get into a fight with these chicks and I gotta get out the car to break it up or help you and the police comes, who do you think goes to jail in this scenario?"* I broke my silence and answered, "You." He continued, *"You damn right me. Two big white chicks, your half-white ass, and my big black ass. I go to jail. Now let me tell you something. I will not protect you when you're wrong. I won't let you get me shot up, beat up, killed, or put in jail because you started shit with someone and because you think it's my job to fight for you as your man. That's not respecting my position as your man; that's taking advantage of it. Now if someone starts shit with you, I got you. But don't you ever do no stupid shit like that again."* I apologized to him and my daughter, and not only did I never do anything like that again, I can now see more clearly what he meant by entitlement and double standards in different situations. I know a typical woman's response might be, "Well he was wrong for stopping the car. He did not have to do that." Sure, but I may have missed the lesson and the next time that happened could have been with a dude with a gun or some other crazy, more dangerous situation. I feel Patrice did the right thing in that situation and took that opportunity to clean up the old project girl's mentality of feeling entitlement towards having her man (or crew) protect her at all costs. That type of bad temper is one that could possibly get everyone killed. Too many women overlook their own responsibility in situations and always put the blame on the man. It is always, "I did this because you did that." But again, Patrice would never allow me to victimize myself, and sometimes the best way to see yourself is not only through situations like this but by observing other people and their entitlement and double standards towards you and the people you love.

One night, Patrice and I we were riding through

downtown Manhattan at a very busy intersection, and we encountered lots of pedestrians attempting to anxiously cross the street prematurely, two of which were a very intoxicated woman and her slightly less intoxicated boyfriend. She decided to start banging on the front right side of the passenger's door of Patrice's Yukon Denali in protest that where he stopped the vehicle was about a half a foot into the crosswalk. With total disregard that she and about one hundred other pedestrians were standing in the street long before the light turned red, she began to scream in our direction. Her rage was clearly directed at Patrice, who was in the driver's side of the car. Her boyfriend, trying to calm her down, was pulling her away as she, with all of her confident rage, was forcing herself and her insults towards the driver's side door to attack. Patrice, with total disregard for her, began yelling out the window to her boyfriend. *"Hey man,"* he said, *"Your girl is gonna get you killed one day."* The boyfriend (speaking over his girlfriend's ranting) was telling her to stop while pulling her away and apologizing to Patrice at the same time. He realized that he was in a very bad situation. Finally, as the couple approached and the irate female calmed down slightly, the boyfriend was able to communicate with Patrice. "Dude," the guy said to Patrice, "I am sorry. She's drunk." Patrice repeated to the guy, *"She's gonna get you killed someday. Why do you let her do that?"* The guy made the drunken excuse for her once again. Patrice began to go into his normal lecture on entitlement and double standards, but the guy interrupted, saying, "Yeah man, I know. I listen to you all the time Patrice. You fucking rule man." As the light changed to green and we began to pull off, and Patrice said, *"Thanks man. Get that bitch in check or leave her at home."* During the rest of the ride, I got to hear the lecture that Patrice wanted to give to them but could not because the light turned green and we pulled off. It was a repeat occurrence of the pasta situation in my head. While it was happening, I could see clearly what she was doing wrong. I also predicted precisely what Patrice was going to say to the guy about how she was going to get him killed before

73

he said it. Although I knew what the entire lecture was going to be about as we rode home, I quietly listened anyway, allowing the danger of entitlement and double standards speech to sink in deeper. Besides, Patrice never did mind talking and repeating lessons, and I did not mind listening to them repeatedly, especially once I thought I had gained enough experience and wisdom to relate to what he was saying on a different level. Instead of it being a lesson for me, it was a lesson for someone else, which felt more like a discussion between two like-minded people. It made me feel more on an equal playing field with him—like a kid who finally matures enough to babysit their younger sibling and has a conversation with their mom when she gets home about how kids do not listen. The more examples I experienced with Patrice, the more I could see things for myself. I was becoming less of a student and more like a peer—which felt very empowering.

In consideration of double standards when it

comes to domestic violence, there are many cases in which the woman was first to strike. If the man retaliates and strikes the woman back, I suppose that could technically be considered equality right? I am sure that most women would never agree to being *that* equal. It is as if many women speak out of both sides of their mouth. If we expect men to have physical restraint, then we as women should respect that repression by offering restraint of our own. It is wrong to operate under the guise that a man cannot do something to you just because you are a woman and take advantage of the rules. Whether written or unwritten, those rules are here to protect women because women are clearly not the dominate being, thus not equal in that sense. If we truly want to find some type of real equality, the first step is to refrain from taking advantage of double standards. In no way am I saying that a man who uses his dominant strength to beat a woman is rightfully doing so because she hit him first. I do not want to be misunderstood, so let me share my first encounter with domestic abuse and take accountability for my actions in creating this particular circumstance.

As mentioned, I was with my high school boyfriend for approximately four years, and for three of those years he was also involved with my best friend, and they eventually had their first child together. The fact that I was hurt on so many levels and all of the specific details of that particular situation are irrelevant to my current point. What is relevant is my actions and attitude after discovering their relationship. At first we broke up, but then we became an on-again, off-again couple, which carried over from twelfth grade into my first year of college. When we were on again, my temperament was volatile.

One day after school, when the betrayal was still fresh, I was at his house visiting and we began to argue. Well, maybe I should say that I began to argue. See, this person who I was in love with and whom I thought was in love with me was very nonchalant about the entire situation and showed little remorse. In fact, it seemed as if he thought it was funny that he was sleeping with two best friends without one of them knowing. I felt foolish and embarrassed. As you can imagine, for a young, insecure high school female, this was devastating. While I was pouring out my heart and pain to him, my rage grew more and more as he basically ignored me and continued watching television. I was standing over him screaming and crying and he was sitting on the edge of his bed, occasionally looking in my direction. I reached in my bag and pulled out my science textbook and started pounding it on the back of his head. That got his attention and he stood up aggressively and told me to stop. I did not stop swinging the book at him, but now he was blocking it. Did I mention earlier that he was a star athlete in football, basketball, and baseball? His massive athletic strength, however, was no match for my rage. At least that's what I thought in my out of control, emotional mind. He kept blocking my strikes until I dropped the textbook, so I started kicking him. He kept telling me to stop as he backed me up out of his room. At this point we were at the top of a staircase, and because I was completely out of control punching and kicking him with all I had in me, I did not even notice. In my mind, I knew he would never hit me back because I was a girl, so I kept striking. He, as I thought, did not hit me back. What I was not prepared for, however, was the most powerful and intense mush to the face of my life. After his last deep breath and telling me to stop, he took me by my face and pushed me so hard I fell face first down the staircase. That fall left me with a swollen, bloody lip, a black eye, and a permanent injury called temporomandibular joint dysfunction. Temporomandibular joint dysfunction, also known as TMJ, is a joint and muscle disorder with problems or symptoms of the chewing muscles and joints that connect your lower jaw to your skull. To this day, my TMJ is a daily reminder that every man has a breaking point, justifiable or not.

Now, am I saying that he had every right to lose control so much that he pushed me face first down the stairs? No, not necessarily. But I will not excuse myself for being out of control either. I did not notice the staircase, so why should I assume he did? We expect a man to walk away. Why do we as women not hold ourselves accountable to walk away as well in these types of situations? Why would I think it is ok to repeatedly smash someone in the back of the head with a large textbook and then start kicking him when he removed the textbook option? Because I am a girl and he hurt my feelings and I know he was raised to never hit a woman? Hard as it may be for us to control our emotions sometimes, we have to look at the probable consequences and never assume that a man won't reach his breaking point and give you a blow that will leave you permanently damaged.

Not only did that leave me physically damaged, it was also the foundation for my next abusive situation, which was purely mental. As I mentioned, we were an on-again, off-again couple after the betrayal—even after the mush to the face. Whenever we were off, I made the classic mistake that a lot of women make: I tried to make him jealous by messing with other guys. I even tried to mess with some of his friends and teammates. I stooped so low that I flirted with and kissed his cousin, who was like a brother to him. It was not until I met Patrice many, many years later that I understood why none of that made him jealous and why all those guys just laughed at me. I was doing what I thought would hurt him because that is what hurt me. But he could care less and just looked at me with even less value, because men do not think like women, they think like men. But, at the time, I did not know that. I just thought I had not picked the right guy that would make him jealous yet. So the next guy I decided to mess with I thought was sure to do the trick. He was the biggest drug dealer in the Pittsburgh area. He had money, power, and respect and would put anybody in check for me. Quite frankly, he was known not just as a drug dealer, but also as a gang-banger and killer. People feared him, and this was now my new fling.

My intentions in this new relationship, of course, were not pure. I was still in love with my high school sweetheart, so my attraction for the new guy was minimal. I did not enjoy him much, but he certainly enjoyed me. After a while, I noticed that he was a bit controlling and probably in love with me a bit too much. Like many other women who find themselves with controlling men, I became afraid of him. He never hit me or was physically aggressive. The fear he instilled was purely mental. He used to plant threatening seeds in my head, telling me that he could not live without me and that if I ever left him he would kill me because he could not bear to see me with another man. I was barely nineteen years old at the time and quite terrified. Of course, instead of recognizing that I foolishly got myself into this situation, I blamed my high school sweetheart for hurting me. If he had not done what he did to me, I would still be with him and not in this new scary situation. Patrice identifies this way of thinking as the way in which women will victimize themselves, leaving themselves unaccountable for their own actions. Of course, when I told my high school boyfriend my reasoning for my new fling, he laughed at me. At this point, we were no longer on again or off again, but we talked on the phone from time to time. So I continued on in my new, uncomfortable relationship with the gang-banging drug dealer, which led me to another physical scar that I also carry with me to this day.

One night at approximately 3 am, he (the drug dealer) drove up to the back of my house and parked in the alley. He called me on the phone and told me to come outside. When I went outside to the car and got in, I could see that he was high on some type of drug. I do not know what type of drug he was on at the time, but he was definitely out of his mind. He had a gun on his lap and began telling me how he was going to kill himself tonight and take me with him. I was so scared, all I could do was smile and say ok to everything he was saying. He kept this up for hours until the sun came up, telling me about all the crazy things he has done, why he doesn't feel like he should live anymore, and why I had to die with him. He was so possessive of me that even if he was dead he did not want me to be with anyone else. It was summertime, and he kept the car windows rolled up the entire time with a tiny crack and no air conditioning. It was hot and very sweaty in the car. Finally, around 9 am, he fully opened the windows and began to drive. He gave me a t-shirt that was in the back seat and told me to wipe my face off and look presentable. I had no clue where we were going and I dared not ask. I just smiled and said, "Ok."

He pulled up to a tattoo parlor that had just opened up in town and we went in. When we walked into the tattoo parlor, it was as if nothing had happened. It was like watching Dr. Jekyll and Mr. Hyde. He was cheerful and friendly to everyone, and it seemed as if he knew everyone in the room. In fact, it appeared as if we had an appointment. He said to one of the tattoo artists, "Yeah, me and my lady are finally going to get our tattoos today." Then he looked at me and said, "Pick out a design." There were tons of tattoo designs all over the parlor walls to choose from, but I just looked up, pointed to the first thing I saw on the wall, and asked, "how about that?" It was a snake wrapped around a heart with a dagger going through it. He said, "That's perfect." So I sat in the chair and received a tattoo on my chest over my heart with the drug dealer's name on the inside as he instructed them to do. I just laid there terrified, deeply disturbed by the fact that not only was I getting a tattoo that I did not want, but it was also going to be in a visible area that I did not choose, with his name—forever.

Every time I hear someone say, well, he did not have a gun to your head when you got the tattoo, I just put my head down in shame. I have not told many people that story. Many people simply think me getting a tattoo was just a bad, rebellious teenage choice. My mother looked at me with great disappointment, and surprisingly, so did my high school sweetheart. Finally, for a second or two, I saw some type of emotion towards me from him. He shook his head and said to me, "You tatted that fools name on you? I thought you were better than that. I've always thought you were even better than me. Like, you would be the one to go somewhere in life. But oh well." Then he laughed at me—again.

I have spent countless dollars and endured painful laser procedures to try and get this tattoo removed, but it is still there. It is faded, but it is still there. I mostly cover it with make-up and have contemplated getting a tattoo to cover it up, but regardless, it is still another scar that I have to live with. It is another lesson in life that taught me that when you do things for the wrong reasons, the consequences could be disastrous.

After that day at the tattoo parlor, the drug dealer and I did not last much longer. He made more threats until one day I did something that I will never forget: I called his bluff. I told him if he was going to kill me, then he should do it. I think I had just watch Quentin Tarantino's movie Reservoir Dogs and had the classic line, "Are you gonna bark all day little doggie, or are you gonna bite?" stuck in my head. He did not kill me, thank God, and our relationship faded away into dust. I do not even claim him as one of my boyfriends of the past. I rarely talk about him or that situation, but I thought it was relevant to share. When I told Patrice this story, he began to clarify possessiveness and ownership to me. He told me that if a gun and intense mental abuse were not a factor, no woman or man should tattoo a person's name on their body. He said that a real man would never require a woman to do that because it's a *"bitch move"* based in insecurity. People have to be secure in their relationships without having to prove their love to one another through extreme measures. True love is

86

accommodating each other's wants, desires, and needs without hurting each other or making the other person feel like they have to prove their love through extreme measures. In actuality, if you are required to do something extreme to prove your love to a person, it is likely that it will not be enough. In fact, it will probably never be enough once you start going down that road, and you will find yourself in a vicious cycle. In this particular situation, I was so afraid of what he might do to me, not only because of his threats, but also because my previous relationship taught me in some ways that if I retaliate, or anger a man to a point of no return, I could be hurt badly. I must admit and be accountable for my participation in this situation, as well as the prior one. I got involved with a known, volatile man, for all the wrong reasons. As a young girl, I blamed everyone except myself. As an adult reflecting on life with intentions of growing and learning, I, with the help of Patrice, was able to see my mistakes and hold myself accountable. Recognizing your own wrongdoing does not excuse the abuse and relieve the other person of their actions. It gives you knowledge and power because now you know what not to do in future relationships. While both of these examples are extreme, neither of these abusive situations is justifiable for anyone involved, including myself.

Both of these relationships set me up with the ingrained awareness that not all men will follow unspoken rules or care to entertain double standards. It made me more cautious and helped me to stop and think twice before making irrational, emotional decisions. But it took Patrice to really outline the dos and don'ts of respect with men. Not only in abusive situations, but also in everyday normal life, women tend to feel it is ok to become less of a wife and more of a mom by giving their man demands grounded in their own feelings and needs. Why is it that women tend to feel so comfortable making men uncomfortable in any given situation? But if men do it to us, it is wrong?

A less dramatic and intense example of double standards as defined by Patrice is his infamous bit that has probably taken place in every office across the globe at some point. In the bit he says, *"Having women work with men is like having a grizzly bear work with fish dipped in honey."* He explains how women will come to work and subtly flirt with a man by giving him an uncomfortable shoulder rub while visiting his desk area or wear provocative and seductive clothing and perfume, but the very second a man responds to any of this, she can (and likely will) take him to the human resources department, where he will possibly be fired. This was all part of the very famous bit from Patrice's Elephant In The Room Comedy Central special, which inspired the infamous holiday, Harassment Day, in which every year, the Tuesday before Thanksgiving, a man gets to make sexual advances at a woman in the work place without being accused of sexual harassment. I cannot say that corporate America has

adopted this holiday just yet, but I do know that hardcore
Patrice fans reach out to me every year in celebration.

It never ceases to amaze me that most women,
even once being shown the light of the truth, will still
take complete advantage of double standards and remain
entitled. Or, is it that we as women are so insensitive to
men that we cannot see the light of the truth and what we
do to contribute to these things? Maybe it is a little bit of
both, but the bottom line is, if men have to restrain, so
should women. Isn't that a better defined way of having
true equality? Even in the case of general conversation
and speech, women feel like they can say anything to a
man: Tell him he needs to work out. Tease him about his
beer belly. But let a man truthfully answer the typical "Do
I look fat in this?" question from his woman and it is
likely that the rest of the day will be spoiled. Typically, a
woman can even gawk at their favorite male celebrity
crush in a sexual tone right in front of their man without
any level of discomfort, but the very second a man does

the exact same, he is bombarded with emotions. When Tiger Woods's infidelities were front-page news and Tiger began to apologize, Patrice pleaded in disgust and posted on Twitter, *"Uh boy! Tiger please STFU! Men gotta stop validating women's notion that wanting to fuck pussy contrary to their own is an illness."* He felt that Tiger should just be honest and say that he loves his wife but probably got married too soon—that he should have had many sexual experiences with many different women before settling down—that wanting sex, and lots of it is not a disease and has nothing to do with how much he loves his wife. But of course, that type of honesty is rare, and most women would have marginalized his truth anyway, so why bother? In fact, most men do not bother. They just shy away and agree to whatever it is that women have decided that they are: Immature. Addicted. Selfish. But, with women who do the same things, there is usually an excuse attached to it that will point in the direction of a man.

Patrice was so special because he not only made very complicated things in our feminine minds simplistic, he also made us laugh about it. However, we cannot just giggle and then shrug our shoulders at the truth and leave it at that. One step in the right direction to not contribute to double standards is to do our part to apply restraint in all areas and be accountable for our own actions. Let's not point fingers. Let's just do our part. Take every situation and flip it before you judge it. If we are understanding of how women can cheat emotionally and why, then we must also be understanding of why men cheat physically. Attention is to a woman, what pussy is to a man. We as women definitely want our cake and we want to eat it too. But, what we need to understand is that men also want their cake and they want to eat their cake as well. As a couple, the best you can do is be open and honest with each other so that you can build trust and have good communication. Men, however, usually have a more practical approach to trust and communication.

*C*hapter 4

*T*ruth & *C*ommunication

"I like who likes me."

— *Patrice O'Neal*

TRUTH & COMMUNICATION

The most difficult thing about the truth is that it arises feelings of guilt, insecurity, shame, embarrassment and, most of all, fear. Truth inspires the fear of being judged and the fear of rejection because of the possibility that others may not accept your truth. These factors inhibit most people so deeply that they even lie to themselves. Patrice, however, was known for his brutal honesty. In fact, he once said that the word brutal should be associated with liars, not honest people. He felt that "brutal liars" are more fatal than a person willing to share and speak the truth. *"Liars don't like me."* He said. *"People who lie—people who live a lie. There are people who love living lies. I was thinking the other day; 'brutal honesty' is a dumb term. The word 'brutal' should be associated with lying, like, 'You're a brutal liar' as opposed to somebody who is just going to inform you of what they believe the truth to be."* While the truth may cut deeply, it offers the opportunity to grow and learn, whereas lies just send you spiraling in circles of never-ending confusion and misery. But some people lie to themselves for so long that they do not even know what the truth is anymore. With women, Patrice felt that most of us never would take full responsibility for our truth, especially in relationships. What we do is generally because of something someone else did first or what we think is socially acceptable, whereas with men, they are more likely to make decisions based on their own individual system of what brings them happiness. That is not to say that men are fearless of being judged, but it is true that men are judged differently.

I personally have always admired a man's ability to be promiscuous guilt free. While there are many women that claim to be able to do as men do and live a promiscuous lifestyle and feel no way about it, I beg to differ with their truth claims that they too can do such things without any shame, guilt, attachment, or fear of being judged because it goes against the very nature of who we are as a female creature. To get me to understand the complexities of the truth in this matter, Patrice would use many different analogies to simplify things to communicate his point of view. To really drive home the points discussed in earlier chapters, let me share with you a few analogies that Patrice used to help communicate the differences between the male and female species.

One of my favorite analogies he used is fish. Patrice loved animals and we had a two-hundred gallon fish tank in our home filled with beautiful African Cichlids. It was the very first thing you would notice when you came into our house. He loved the fish and felt that fish were useful in relaxing as well as relating. To describe the type of men women usually are attracted to and why, he used the great white shark. As with humans, there are male great white sharks and there are female great white sharks. In the dating game, Patrice said that most men tend to stay in their league with their type. Meaning, most male sharks seek female sharks and desire them, whereas some women think to themselves, *"I hate the way male sharks treat female sharks, so I am now going to date these penguins or seals who look at me and run in fear. I am gonna catch one and I am not gonna eat it, but I am just gonna play around with it and have this weaker animal who looks at me with fear and reverence."* This analogy explains how some women that are insecure and have power issues seek to date a man who would be considered weaker. These type of women think, *"I am not gonna sit here and deal with other sharks."* However, after dating the penguins or seals for a while, it gets to a point where she will begin to despise these weak men because she challenges him all day, treats him like garbage, and he just lets her dominate the relationship and do anything she wants to him. So in order to feel like a woman, she has to find another shark and apply her natural shark instinct to try and challenge him like she does with the penguins or seals. But the male shark will not allow her to dominate him. He stays in his top-of-the-food-chain position, where she swims alongside his power. A woman with an out-of-control ego and power issues has trouble standing beside her man because of fear of his dominance. This is out of order.

Since Patrice understood what type of "shark" he was dealing with in me, he needed to get me to understand what type of shark I was dealing with in him. In order for us to be happy, he needed me to respect the things that he was doing to go against his nature to accommodate the things that I needed, like cheating. Understanding the concept of cheating as a natural instinct to hunt and "catch fish" Patrice used the analogy of sport fishing to communicate this idea to me and to the world. He explained, *"I just want my girl to know that my natural instincts stopped once I said I love her. I made a decision to be a 'good guy.' I know that fucking a lot of women is bad for her. She don't want it. She wants commitment and she wants monogamy, and I give it to her and I just want her to know that— I want her to value the sacrifice. All I want is for women to understand what we are. We want a lot of fucking women. It's like being a fisherman; you go out there and try to catch fish. You catch the fish and you show it to your friends, you take a picture, you look at it, and you throw it back in the water. Your girl is a fish that jumped back on the boat after you threw it in the water. Because*

you caught her, she keeps jumping back on your boat. Usually some

fish get the idea; they swim back into the ocean and hope you come

back again to catch them, but the fish that's in your life was just

flapping around your boat. She ran all the other fish off. At some

point you tell her, 'Look, my job is to catch fish.' And she goes

'What the fuck, is that all I am to you?' And as a man that has

this dichotomy, you say, 'No, no I am not a piece of shit. You're the

last fish. I wanted to catch you.' Now you're dating and in love and

your girl say, 'Now that you love me, why do you still have your

boat? And why do you still have your pole and all your bait?' And

you say, 'So, are you saying you want me to stop being what I was

to get you?' What that means, when I stop being what I am, you

start to look at me and say, 'You ain't even got a boat, that guy has

a boat, you used to be this great fisherman.'"

Sounds like a catch twenty-two situation to the

untrained ear, but what Patrice is really trying to teach us

here is that if a man is doing his best to go against his

nature, all he usually wants in return is appreciation and

respect. Unfortunately, not all of us are gifted with the ability to communicate the truth though charm and simplified analogies like Patrice. I remember the first analogy that cut my soul to the core as a woman, but it was eye opening and I will always appreciate receiving this particular bit of truth medicine.

As a young woman who was constantly told how very pretty she was her entire life, there was nothing to prepare me to someday meet a man who would not only tell me that my prettiness was not that important, but that the value of it was also decreasing.

"An ugly 19 year old is prettier than a fine ass 40 year old." – Patrice O'Neal

I was in my late twenties when I met Patrice. I had already had my daughter and was dealing with hiding my not-so-perfect body after my skin was destroyed. If you name a spot on a woman's body where she might get stretch marks during pregnancy that is where you will find them on me. The stretch marks went from my breasts to my hips and all the way down to my inner and outer thighs and calves. There was nothing left untouched. My breasts were empty, and my stomach was ravaged with so much loose skin and so many stretch marks that Patrice called it lasagna. When I say my breasts were empty, I want you to picture those third-world pictures of women who look like they fed an entire African village with their breast milk and were left with long, saggy breasts with no meat inside—just loose skin. That was my body after pregnancy. I was so insecure and depressed that I began my mission of plastic surgery. First stop was breast implants. I basically told the doctor to just fill them in to where there were. No bigger, no smaller. I was not the type to ever want cosmetic surgery prior to my pregnancy, but now, I was on a mission to get back to the prettiness of the past that I once had. At the time, I could not afford to fix all of my body issues, just my breasts. In fact, I really could not afford to fix my breasts either, but between my sister Michelle's good credit and my own, somehow we came up with $10,000 to pay for my new boobies. This was about a year or so before I met Patrice.

When I met Patrice, without him knowing my back story or even seeing the rest of what I considered a disastrous body after my pregnancy under my clothes, Patrice labeled me with "pretty girl syndrome" and decided to help me find a way to rise above my prettiness, and without knowing it at the time, I would be learning to accept myself, flaws and all. But how does one begin to teach such things to a young woman who has identified her only value in her appearance her whole life? According to Patrice, you teach her how to develop a good jump shot.

"Women age like bread, not like wine." – Patrice O'Neal

The first analogy that he used that cut to my core was a sports analogy. Being from Pittsburgh, I have always loved sports, so Patrice used a lot of sports analogies to help me understand and grow. We both loved basketball; he was a Boston Celtics fan and I a New York Knicks fan, so you can just imagine those arguments on game day. I would scream at him with all this passion but had no real basis for what I was saying. After all, I never played any sports and did not really study the game much. I just enjoyed it and knew the basics. So Patrice told me he was going to teach me to watch basketball intelligently so that we could have better arguments. That he did, and it made me love and appreciate the game even more. The sports analogy that he used to get me to understand what he meant by "Women age like bread, not like wine" was ingenious because it did not attack me personally and all of my insecurities and body issues directly. It hit me at my core as a woman. He said to me, "*Look Von, your almost 30, and in order to stay in the game, your gonna have to develop a mean jump shot.*" He continued by using one of the greatest basketball players to ever live as an example: Michael Jordan. "*When Michael Jordan was young, he was unstoppable. He could dunk on you from damn near half court. That dunk is like a woman's prettiness. When a woman is young and bouncing around with all her youngness, she doesn't have to develop any other skills, like being easy going, considerate, respectful, fun, and charming: all the things that men have to develop during adolescence. But as a woman gets older, much like when Jordan started getting old and his knees started hurting, in order to keep playing, he developed a mean jump shot. Most women are never told to develop a jump shot, so they are bouncing around at 30 and 40 with jump shot prettiness, trying to dunk like the 20 year old girls, and that is why they will lose the game. The older women that stay in the game are the ones who learn to have value outside of their prettiness. Now, as a woman, you should always make an effort to keep yourself as pretty as possible as you get older, but you cannot win on prettiness alone. You have to develop a jump shot. Become more valuable than just your vagina. Learn to be pleasant and likeable.*"

He could not have said it better. That analogy will stay with me for the rest of my life, but it is admittedly a constant struggle. Acceptance of oneself is a battle every day. Not hiding what you are is difficult for all of us on many levels. It is not as if the very day Patrice gave me that analogy I was able to accept myself and the hardcore truth that not only is age catching up to me, but my once-perfect body is a few years removed from me and it is not coming back. But that did not mean I would not still try.

Now that the boobies were taken care of, I dreamt of the day I would find a solution to remove my stretch marks and lasagna. That answer came the day I received a $30,000 settlement from a car accident that left me with a permanent neck injury. At the time, Patrice was doing ok financially, and my bartending job wasn't too shabby either, so when I got the settlement, I wanted to splurge on myself a bit. After all, if I was going to be left with this pain in my neck for the rest of my life, the least I could do was treat myself to fix other areas of my body that caused me some type of pain, even if it was just mental. So I discussed with Patrice what I wanted to do with the money. I told him I wanted to first get Lasik eye surgery (I had been wearing glasses and contacts since first grade and everything that was more than one inch from my face was always a blur). In addition, I wanted to get liposuction and a tummy tuck to help smooth out the stretch marks in my hip and thigh areas, and of course, I wanted to get rid of the lasagna. Patrice said, *"It* (the stretch marks and lasagna) *doesn't bother me, but do what you want to do."* That was the beauty of being in a relationship with a strong man like Patrice. Even if he disagreed with something, he never *made* me do anything. He knew that sometimes people just have to do what they have to do to make themselves happy or at least make an attempt to find their happiness. So I did it. I got my Lasik surgery and had 20/20 vision; to this day I feel that is the best money I ever spent. The cosmetic surgery on my legs and stomach, well, that's a different story.

Getting a tummy tuck and liposuction on my legs was the worse pain I have ever been through, second only to childbirth. But, Patrice was there every step of the way. He took me to the hospital to get the surgery, and when I started getting nervous and scared as they pulled me away to start the process of putting me under anesthesia, he simply said, *"See you when you're done"* and patted me on the arm. His nonchalance at my fear and paranoia of possibly dying during surgery comforted and calmed me, and when I was done, he was right there when I woke up. I woke up in the worst pain. The people in the hospital were not too accommodating or helpful, and before I get too deep into that, I will just tell you what Patrice's take on that was. He said, *"Look sweetie, there are people in this hospital dying that don't want to. You chose to be in this pain, so (not that it's right, but) some of these nurses just don't give a fuck about your beauty woes."*

I could not wait to get home. When I was released from the hospital, I was still in a lot of pain, but now I was home with someone who did care. Patrice basically nursed me back to health. He took care of me while I was in the bed in pain. He made me homemade soup and helped me get in and out of the bed to go to the bathroom. He helped to wash me every day and made sure I took my medicine and pain killers at the right times. He also drove me to and from all of my follow-up appointments and made me laugh even when I wanted to cry. And when it was all said and done and I was all healed, I still was not back to that young twenty-something body that I had been dreaming of. My stretch marks were still very prominent, and the liposuction on my thighs left dents that looked like cellulite (cellulite that was not there before the surgery). And although the tummy tuck removed all of the lasagna, I now had a scar that spanned from hip to hip across my lower belly. Patrice called that my Wonder Woman belt.

My cosmetic ventures now left me on another mission: to fix what I was left with from the surgery.

Although I live with the Michael Jordan jump shot analogy in my head and was working on becoming better at accepting myself, I still wanted my prettiness back. I was still ashamed of my body. I just wanted to find a way to get my confidence back, and with one statement from Patrice, I had an epiphany and found my way.

One day, long after I had healed from my cosmetic surgery, I was plotting and planning what type of tattoo I could get to cover up the Wonder Woman belt that was now spanning across my lower belly. I asked Patrice's opinion, and he told me he thought tattoos were stupid. I of course already knew that, so I asked him again. "I know you think they are stupid," I said, "but I have to do something about this scar." Patrice looked at me and said, "*When are you going to stop? You keep covering one scar with another scar, and with another scar, and another. When are you going to stop?*" and walked away. He went into the living room and turned on the TV and left me to ponder my actions. I knew not to push him any further once he left me in the bedroom alone to think about what he just said, and I did not want to press the issue any further. What he said hit me so hard. It was as if he put a mirror of truth in front of me yet again. He was right. I kept trying to hide my truth instead of really accepting it and working with what I had left to "stay in the game" so to speak. I began to realize even further that if I kept trying to operate in this world by living backwards with what I used to be, I would never become who I was supposed to be. That day changed my life and gave me more confidence as an older, scarred-up woman than I ever had as a perfectly proportioned, even-toned, smooth-bodied young girl, and I will always cherish that moment. I also realized in that moment that while Patrice used to rub my lower belly and even sleep and cuddle with me in that position when the lasagna was there, he never touched my lower belly after the surgery. Patrice made it clear that my imperfections did not bother him, but he knew I had to find my own way. Otherwise, I would have had him to blame for my unhappiness if I chose to not have the surgery. Sometimes we fix things that we think will make us more attractive to men, when it's really our imperfections that they love.

Patrice instilled so much strength in me through utilizing life-changing truth and communication of logic and reasoning; however, I must say, the battle in a woman's mind between logic and her emotions will always be an ongoing war. In order to succeed in rising above your emotions and ingrained entitlement, as well as making an effort to not take advantage of double standards as a woman, you must dig deep into the understanding of logic versus your emotions.

Chapter 5

Logic vs. Emotions

"Ain't nothing wrong with washing a brain if it's dirty."

— *Patrice O'Neal*

LOGIC vs. EMOTIONS

Arguably the most challenging aspect of being a woman is to be able to accomplish rational thinking above our emotions, especially once a month when our natural hormonal chemical imbalances spins everything in our minds, bodies, souls, *and relationships* out of control. No excuses, but it is a proven scientific fact that during menstrual cycles, women struggle with something that men will never fully understand. Quite frankly, most women do not fully understand the dynamics of what goes on within our bodies and minds during that time of the month either. But our emotional woes are not just a monthly struggle.

As a woman, we are structured to be emotional beings. This is great in some aspects, since we are by nature the caregivers and nurturers of the family; however, if we do not gain an understanding of our emotions and some type of control over them, we can be the cause of the destruction of the family (and every relationship that we have both personally and professionally for that matter). So, until we recognize and accept that we are in fact emotional beings with ongoing emotional battles inside of us daily, we will always be on the more frustrating side of the tracks in our relationships. We should not use what we are and how we are structured as an excuse as to why we do things. We have to challenge ourselves to think above our emotions and into a logical place, which, admittedly, is easier said than done.

Patrice loved to challenge his audiences, friends, family, and even strangers in the mall or the grocery store with his philosophies. No one was off limits, especially me. If you were to ever try and debate or argue with any of his points, or engage in any type of conversation with him, he would insist that you have a really solid, well-thought-out retort or some type of point to make. Phrases like, "just because" or "because that's just what I think" or "I don't know" were all unacceptable answers.

If you could not give a solid, well-thought-out answer, then he would keep drilling you until you either submitted to his point of view, walked away crying, or actually came up with a well-thought-out answer. During my time with Patrice, I experienced all three, but when I finally stopped walking away and crying, I realized that he was making me stronger. He was exercising my brain and strengthening my tolerance. Talking and debating with Patrice was like lifting weights, but a bit more exhausting I dare to say. The best part about engaging in such tiring conversations and debates, however, was that they forced me to listen and think past my emotions. Whenever I found myself submitting to Patrice because I could not find any reasonable response to what he was saying, that is where I began to find my growth. I realized this by discovering that in submitting, I was forced to listen to reason regardless of my emotional opinion, and that is where the real truth existed.

"Women want us to like them, but they don't even

like each other" —Patrice O'Neal

One of my favorite examples of this begins with a

short but sharp statement that Patrice would make often

to me, audiences, friends, family, etc.: *"We're* (men) *better*

than you." Of course, as a woman, that statement will

immediately feel insulting and put you in defense mode,

ready to fight and argue. That was Patrice's technique

with women in general. He knew that in order to really

get a woman to listen to him, he had to shock her

emotions. He did just that by saying *"We're better than you"*

to set up one of the greatest hypothetical scenarios I have

ever heard to prove a point.

If you were one of the many women who heard

Patrice say this, and you defended it, then you know he

certainly offered you a chance to argue your point

rationally. He would say, *"Ok ladies, hypothetically speaking, if*

you died and went to heaven and God told you he was going to reincarnate you and send you back to Earth as the opposite sex, but you have the option of changing anything you want about the opposite sex that you want to change before he sends you back, what would you change? I can tell you what men would change. You (women) have periods every month. You have to bear children in pain. You worry constantly about everything. Your love is even a burden because you never have peace. You can't have genuine fun or sex without guilt. You have to sit down to pee. Everything you are as a species is designed for you to slow down or ask for help. If a man has to come back to Earth as a woman, we are changing all of that. Now, what would you change about a man?" In the still, dead silence as the audience (or individual) is trying to think of something she would change about a man, Patrice interjects and says, *"I'll tell you what you would change. Nothing. You wouldn't change anything about a man. We are the shit. We are stronger than you, we are cooler than you, we are not burdened like you, and the only pain we really have to live with is dealing with you muthafuckers."* With all ego, hurt feelings, and defensiveness aside, I honestly had to agree with Patrice when he first laid this scenario out to me. As

117

painful as that scenario may be for women to hear and admit to, it's actually hilariously true. If you have the ability to calm down and not walk away or get so angry that it brings you to tears, you will realize the significance and it will make you stronger. If you are filled with tears and walk away, what that signifies is that you really do agree, but it hurts your feelings and you have no retort. With that response, you are simply revealing that you are shocked and hurt by what was revealed to you, and that is the truth. The truth is, most women would not change anything about being a man if they were presented with the reincarnation option from God. Being enlightened with facts will open the door to acceptance of what and who you are—both good and bad.

I used to have people verbally attacking me because of Patrice's logic and reasoning when it comes to domestic relationships and his opinions on women. To a great extent, I still deal with those attacks today. Some of the attackers accuse me of being brainwashed, but I certainly agree with Patrice's statement that there is *"nothing wrong with washing a brain if it's dirty"*—dirty as in misguided, confused, and without direction, which is exactly what I was before I met Patrice in terms of relationships. I, like many women, would have certain feelings without being able to explain exactly what they were, why I had them, and where they were coming from. If I felt strongly about something because it triggered my emotions deeply, then I would likely just blurt out my thoughts without consideration that I could be wrong. The idea that I might be acting irrationally in those situations rarely crossed my mind. The outcome was usually negative and left me pondering why I could not get my point across to the other person. Likely, it was because I really did not have a solid point to go along with my extreme emotions.

If you can learn to think above your emotions and in a logical place, you are likely to not only have a successful relationship with your man, parents, children, friends, co-workers, and even strangers, but you will also find peace of mind for yourself. This is not to say that whatever you feel is not valid and it should be ignored. It is to say that you have to recognize that just because you feel strongly about something emotionally, that does not make you right. Especially when dealing with your man. The first step is admitting that you are an emotional creature. The second step is having empathy towards your man—he just might be right despite how any given situation is making you feel. Or, you can choose to let your ego and emotions stand in your way and take your man down the road of misery with you (which he will ultimately leave), or you can choose to fight through those emotions and find common happiness with him. For me, I chose to take the happy road and became a student of logic.

At the very beginning of every relationship, women have to understand that yes, we will likely be ready for a commitment before the man, so we have to live in what Patrice referred to as "the matrix" until time has closed the door on the many things that make us uncomfortable, like other women. The matrix is a direct reference to the movie in which you have an option in choosing your reality. One of Patrice's favorite's songs was called "Just Be Good To Me." by the S.O.S. Band. Patrice said that the lyrics of this song are a perfect description of how women should be, especially in the beginning of a relationship, and felt that it should be every woman's anthem. The lyrics describe a woman who is in love with a man despite what other people say or think. She only concentrates on how good he makes her feel and how he treats her when they are together. She refuses to allow outside influences or even her own imagination to contradict how well this man treats her when she is with him.

When you first meet a guy, you have to know that he likely already has other women in his life, just as you may have other men. It may be likely that you do not, but is very unlikely that he doesn't. Women have to take time for themselves at certain points in life to refocus, concentrate on school and/or career, and usually during this time will eliminate men and dating from the picture. Why? It is because our natural instinct to care for our men and build a family might serve as a distraction from our own goals. Many women can relate to putting their man above themselves; they fall into being a support system to his goals, and put their own personal goals on the back burner. Men, on the other hand, are quite the opposite. While building himself, he may find that spending time with women (sex) helps to relax him and further inspire him to reach his goals. However, when it comes to commitment, marriage and children, lots of men do not even want to consider it until they are established. Either way, you have to accept that in the beginning growth period with a man there will most likely be other women.

If you like a man and you think he is attractive and charming, then you can go ahead and assume that there are many other women who feel the exact same way about him that you do. Patrice used to tell me, if you ask a man how many women he has and he says none, then he probably has three to five that he is juggling but not claiming. Further, he said that if you ask a man how many women he has and he says one, then it is likely that he is being honest and you at least know where you stand. It is likely that this one woman in his life is high up as far as levels go; yet he is not fully satisfied or committed. Or you can guess that maybe they are new to each other, in which case he is keeping his options open and not fully committed to that one woman just yet. Just because a man is dating multiple women, it does not make him a dog or a player. That makes him honest about where he is in life. If he is not ready to commit or if he has not yet decided with whom he wants to commit, seeing multiple women is not only ok, but it is natural. At the very least, you now know where you stand in the mix, and yes, there is always a mix. Of course, you can never really tell if a person is telling you the absolute truth, but what you can do is set a man up to feel comfortable in telling you the truth. Never ask a man questions with the underlying intention of making him feel bad about his truth and ultimately trying to change it (especially in the beginning). You want him to know that you accept where he is in life and would like the opportunity to grow with him, as you want him to grow with you in your life. If you really think about it, no woman or man is usually ready to commit right away, but many women are willing to force it just to land the relationship, sometimes even going so far as to lie about their interests. Women lie to get relationships, just like men lie to get sex. Either way, that relationship is over before it starts, simply because when each person's true colors emerge, they will discover the truth of how incompatible they really are for each other.

It is not reasonable to expect to just kick down the door of a man's life and immediately start changing his system around because you feel a little jealous and maybe a little insecure about the other women that he is dating. All of us want to feel like we are number one and special, but trust me when I tell you, it feels a lot better when it is earned and not forced. Besides, if you really enjoy this man, I bet it is because he makes you feel really special when he is with you, so focus just on that until you naturally grow into a higher position in his life. That is the matrix. Patrice would always say *"If you dig, you will find, so stay in the matrix of what makes you feel good and how I treat you when you are with me."* But of course it is hard to keep the inner dialogue out of my emotional brain that triggers that bad butterfly feeling in my heart and gut that makes me feel awful every time I imagine that he is saying similar things to another woman. But ladies, it is what it is, especially in the beginning. A man is not going to burn his little black book (so to speak) just because he has chemistry with you. He has to see your consistency with him. Men like to take their time learning each woman while having fun with whoever is providing the different types of happiness that he desires, until one woman eventually becomes the one that fills in all the different desires in his life. In the meantime, you have to be honest with yourself and learn his needs and desires. If he is clear that he needs a woman who cooks for him, for instance, and you hate to cook, then quite frankly, he is not your match. Do not paint the wrong picture and try to cook for him in the beginning knowing that it is not something that you plan to do for him on a consistent basis over time. It is what it is. Move on.

There was a point where Patrice and I had grown so far in our relationship that he said, *"My woman is worth at least five different bitches in my life."* Meaning, he does not have to cheat because I fulfill every area in which he would seek a different need from another woman. But that high level of companionship took time. Years, to be exact, and in the beginning, I had to stay in the matrix and fight off all scenarios in my head whether they were imagined or real. The fact is, in the beginning, men have to protect their options, or what Patrice would call their *"human resource department."*

Patrice taught me to think of a man's system and how he operates it as a corporation. Just like in a real company, every woman that enters his life (corporation) starts out in the same position with opportunity for growth. They all, including me, started out in the mailroom. But to get promoted all the way up the corporate ladder to vice president, one level below the president/CEO, is something that is earned over time and through training and consistent effort—in other words, by learning your man. Just like you cannot walk into a business and demand the highest position without earning it, you cannot walk into a man's life and demand the highest position. No matter how you feel about it, the fact is, you are starting out in the mailroom, and there are one or two women (maybe more) that are in that mailroom as well, or on levels higher than you in his company simply because they have been around longer learning his system. But as long as he is just dating these women and has not given away the coveted vice president title (girlfriend or fiancé), then you have the chance to climb the ladder and pass some of those ladies up in promotions. Your advancement depends on your dedication and work ethic in learning your position. For me, that is exactly how my relationship grew with Patrice. Whenever I used to ask him how I became his woman and why he got rid of all of the others, he would say, *"You hung around,"* meaning I withstood the test of time and patience in growing and being promoted at every level, and I was proven to be compatible with his system and desires. I began to fulfill all of his needs in every position to the point where I could run the company alongside him at the highest level as a partner and co-owner of his company (wife).

It took a long time of building and growing on my part to get to such a high position, as it would in any company. I actually never really understood why men felt the need to keep so many women in their life until Patrice explained the corporation analogy to me, but it wasn't until I started dealing with women during our threesomes phase that it really started to sink in and make sense. During that phase, I learned how unreliable, difficult, and annoying women could be at times. I will explore that in more detail in the next chapter when we talk about sex, but for now, just know that when you are in the beginning of a relationship with a man, he does not know yet that you can fulfill every duty within his company, and there are other women around that are doing their jobs well. That does not mean that you cannot climb the ladder and find other women dropping off and quitting due to lack of promotion (attention) or getting let go and fired from their position because he gave you an opportunity to perform their job and you did it better. These positions can be anything in his life, from sex to cooking and cleaning, to helping him organize his bills. Every man's needs vary, and that is what is so great about the beginning learning process. Not every man requires you to do the same thing, just as every woman has different desires and needs from a man. In no way am I saying that everyone should operate under the same guidelines or follow what society says is good as far as gender roles are concerned. For instance, since Patrice loved to cook and that was not something he needed from a woman, any female that thought she would win him over with a good home-cooked meal was in for a surprise.

I know as a woman reading this you may feel like being defensive reading about the corporation analogy. If you are feeling that way right now, that is great. Take a moment right now to understand that it is your ego and emotions disabling you from growing and understanding, not your rational side that understands this system. To help you get past your ego and emotions right now, let's simply reverse everything. Women are doing the same thing men do in the beginning of relationships, except they may put a guy with a lot of potential that they really like in a higher position within their corporation than he actually deserves. If you are a single woman, you may in fact keep a few guys around to supply your needs. We call that guy "Mr. Right Now." You might have your sex guy or your handyman guy that you keep in the friend zone, your church buddy, or maybe a long-distance text buddy. The list can go on forever, but women seem to forget about all of those guys when they find someone that they want to grow with in a real relationship. In addition to forgetting about all of those guys, we assume the new "Mr. Right" feels the same about us and sometimes insist that he also jump the gun and fire all of his employees in his corporation right away. Well, be rational for him and for yourself. No matter how much potential he has, he should start out in your mailroom as well. No need to jump the gun on either end. He's very unlikely to jump the gun and promote you right away no matter how much potential you have because he is likely using logic to drive his decisions, not his emotions. The best thing to do is spend some time getting to know each other and learn each other's system. Really get to know if you even want to work for each other's company.

Another good example of logic versus emotions is Patrice's comparison to a man's desire to sleep with other women to a woman's menstrual cycle. Much like we have our monthly PMS breakdowns in which we expect our men to show empathy and understanding, we have to also in return empathize with their "period" as well. Patrice used to identify a man randomly being in a bad mood with being faithful. He said that if a man comes home and is in a bad mood and doesn't want to be bothered with you, he may have just turned down the opportunity to be with another woman that he normally would not have turned down if he was single. Therefore, he is cranky. He referred to that as his period. If you think about it rationally, that seems to be a fair comparison. However, a typical response from a defensive woman with her ego and emotions in the forefront is to immediately feel offended and hurt that he was interested in being with another woman, as opposed to recognizing and appreciating that he passed on that woman of interest.

Let us take a moment to explore this situation in our minds. Imagine a man comes home in a cranky mood and his woman insists on him telling her what is wrong. If he answered truthfully and said, "Well, Betty at work was flirting with me all day and wanted to hang out for drinks. She had on a real short skirt and slipped in the fact that she wasn't wearing panties. My dick was hard all day, so I squeezed one out in the car after work in the back alley. I imagined fucking her in the bathroom of whatever local bar we would go to for drinks while I was masturbating, and although it felt good, I sure would like to know how good she gives head and how wet her pussy can get on my dick. But I knew it would hurt you if I cheated, so, like I said, I just masturbated to the thought of it then I came home. I love you, so I did not want to cheat on you, but that makes me feel restricted, and in some ways, old. That feeling put me in a bad mood, so I just need a minute. What's for dinner?"

How do you think this woman would react to his man truth? How would you honestly respond to that dose of truth yourself? Would you tell him you understand and give him a big hug while thanking him for not cheating? Or would you become offended and start a dramatic nagging argument, as if you did not just secretly masturbate to your favorite celebrity that morning after he left for work? Or maybe you masturbated to that gorgeous coworker of yours, or your trainer at the gym. It actually doesn't matter who your fantasy is, you did exactly what he did, but as a woman, you probably feel threatened, hurt, and will likely refuse to admit that it is really not a big deal that he fantasized and desired another woman.

Admittedly, it is hard to fight those immediate emotions of insecurity and jealousy when we hear man truth. I understand that as a woman, when we do certain things, we feel it is harmless because we know no matter what, we are not going to cheat and disrespect our man. We have to allow for the option in our minds that our men may feel the exact same way we do about it and allow him that freedom without judgment. Patrice used to tell me that men do not always want to physically have sex with another woman. They just want to feel like they can. Sometimes, they can find pleasure in just talking about it and not actually doing it. So, let us reconsider the Betty situation. If we stop and take a deep breath and allow ourselves to think rationally above our emotions, we will find that our first thought is acknowledgement of a good man. He came home and did not cheat. If you ever find yourself in that type of scenario and you don't feel gratitude for the fact that he suppressed his natural instincts and did not act out his desires for Betty, then you are delivering blows to his desire to want to not cheat on you. The next time he is presented with the opportunity, he will engage with Betty in the bathroom instead of coming home to his ungrateful nag.

The best part about being with a man like Patrice is that while he was always dishing out his truth and helping me to think logically above my emotions, he was also very supportive and nonjudgmental about whatever my truth was as well. The best thing two people can do for each other is accept that we are just living life as imperfect human beings with natural thoughts and desires that may not always make each other comfortable. Living in truth, having good communication, and being a rational, logical thinker will naturally increase love and respect for one another, and issues with entitlement and double standards will become minimal. I was always able to be myself with Patrice and vice versa, which made me very happy. The more he made me happy, the more I wanted to reciprocate that happiness by giving and sharing in his ultimate desires, which sometimes included sex with a few different Bettys.

Chapter 6

Sex, Trust, & Jealousy

"Women have to like you to sleep with you. Men have to like you to sleep with you again."

— *Patrice O'Neal*

Patrice once described me as a lesbian who just so happens to love him. This is one area in which he eventually grew to understand that he was absolutely, one-hundred-percent wrong. As he discovered through our experiences together, I am a woman that is only interested in engaging in bisexual acts when it is in association with a man. I never had the desire to have a woman as a girlfriend, wife or life partner, or anything outside of regular friendship. Any physical interest in women that I had felt more like a fetish to me than anything else. My interest was directly related to experiencing pleasure by pleasing, particularly the man. To put it quite frankly, whatever turns on my man gets me hot. I am a woman who absolutely adores men; I am quite aware that my desire to please a man may extend beyond what most women would find acceptable, and that is ok. My personal desires to cater to Patrice's every need (as he did mine) did in fact include being open to his desires for other women physically. Ironically, engaging in threesomes with Patrice became something that actually brought us closer and taught me more about men than I ever expected.

In dealing with women and experiencing the inconsistencies and unreliability of women in the dating game, I started to really understand why men keep three to five women in their dating rotation. From women cancelling dates at the last minute to having females catch feelings and start making demands, and everything in between, I began to see just what men meant about our crazy quirks as women that make us very annoying creatures. Patrice would laugh at my impatience about pursuing and dating women. He, of course, was used to the game, whereas I was utterly annoyed. I also became very clear about the primary physical aspect of it all and why sometimes men do not even need to know (or remember) our names. It is because sex is just that: sex. Men do not attach all of their emotions to the physical act of sex, whereas most women certainly do have an emotional connection. Men keep their emotions very separate from their penis and have to build over time to like a woman, and eventually love her. Women are usually invested in some way from the beginning. However, in this odd role of reversals for me, I was looking at these women purely as visual and sexual objects. I had no interest in any of them past a sexual experience with Patrice, which is quite frankly what many men experience when they first meet any woman he is interested in dating. Remember, they have to grow to like and love you gradually, and there is no particular time frame for that growth. He may like you right away after talking with you because he may notice that you have some characteristics that are in tune with what he is looking for, but again, do not expect him to get rid of his rotation of women and jump the broom with you immediately. He will likely be taking his time to get to know you to see if he wants to be in a relationship with you, but he does not need any time to know that he wants to have sex with you. With women, it is usually the opposite. We tend to not take a lot of time emotionally to see if we want a relationship with him because we have the crazy idea that we can "fix" whatever it is we do not like about him, whereas we will take our time giving him sex as a means of holding him off from moving on too quickly. After all, once he has gotten sex from you, what do you have to bargain with—your personality? Such is only the case if you have learned to become far more valuable than just your vagina.

"Pussy ain't all we want, unless that's all you got." –

Patrice O'Neal

When dealing with women in these threesome situations, it seemed like Patrice and I had to jump through hoops just for the *possibility* of her being with us sexually. The arrogance and entitlement of these women made most of them highly unlikeable, but we would tolerate it just for the possibility of sex. Once sex happened, the interest was completely gone. I imagine that is what happens in a one-on-one situation all the time. Men tolerate our nonsense for sex, and then we wonder why we can't get a hold of them after we give it up. It is most likely because you were not very likeable along the way.

I developed such empathy for men through these experiences, and it certainly made my relationship with Patrice much stronger—not only because I was able to supply his desires for what he called "new pussy," but because it also gave me an inside look into how and why men view us in certain ways. Now, I certainly do not mean to suggest to anyone that they should do anything that they are uncomfortable with to grow their relationship, because I most certainly did not. My general interest in threesomes and what I call my bisexual tendencies just enable me to supply a need and desire that my man had. But if you do not have those tendencies, then do not mistake what I am saying and do things that you will regret or resent your man as if he made you engage in things that make you uncomfortable. In fact, not every man wants to engage in threesomes, so you have to work on truth and communication with your man first so that you both know what the other's desires are and if you can honestly accommodate each other's needs. Remember, do not try to change him, and do not change yourself. That does not work. What works is finding someone whose interests and desires match. The only way to find out if that person is a match is to be honest with them about yourself and make the other person very comfortable in being honest about themselves to you by being non-judgmental on both ends. If you do find someone with similar sexual desires or interests but you withhold those experiences from your mate out of jealousy or insecurity, then that is where you are wrong. That is the mistake that many women make very often, as discussed in prior chapters. We want our man to sacrifice many things for us on every level, but when it comes to what we will do to sacrifice for them, we sometimes do not feel it is necessary. We marginalize their desires and

143

try to change them. Again, I want to stress that I am not saying that every woman should engage in threesomes to keep her man, but I am saying that if that is something that he needs and cannot live without, and it is not something that you are comfortable with doing, then 2 + 2 = 4 and you two are probably not meant to be with each other. There are men who do not want to engage in threesomes but may want to have anal sex, or tie you up, or maybe he has a foot fetish. The list of sexual needs and desires can go on forever, but the point I am trying to make is that sex, and all its freaky little details in your partner's mind (and yours), are not exempt from the things necessary to make your relationship a success. Some people think that it is childish and immature to not be with a man because he does not fulfill you sexually, but I say it is quite the opposite. It takes a very mature man or woman to know themselves and know what they need out of a relationship on every level, including sex. Sex is a natural desire, and it is something that you should expect to receive from your partner with total provisions.

144

Otherwise, you will seek to get those needs, whatever they are, elsewhere. Knowing what you want is key, and discussing it with your partner openly without judgment, fear, or insecurity is the first step to getting your needs met or finding out that the person that you are with may or may not be a match for you.

So, why did Patrice feel that I was a lesbian that just so happened to fall in love with him? Well, it is my understanding that he was basing that off of my initial curiosity in being with a woman sexually, which was very extreme. I understood why he would think that, but did not let it distract me from telling him the truth. You have to be confident when you tell the truth and let it unfold. I did not hide my interests from Patrice for fear that he would not believe that I was not a full-blown lesbian. Sometimes people will not believe your truth right away, but that is out of your control. I knew for myself that my curiosity for women was not strong enough for me to pursue it past the idea of it being attached to a man,

145

particularly with Patrice; I was confident that time would confirm that for me, and it did. The more we talked about it, the more intense the interest became. I was excited at his excitement, and he began to recognize that. Words cannot explain how pleasurable it was for me to see him get off on another woman. Not only because I just like watching, or living vicariously through him, but also because it made him happy.

Reciprocation is something in life and relationships that is highly underrated. In my relationship with Patrice, reciprocation flowed naturally. He made me very happy by getting to know me, and I did my best to do just the same. For instance, he would get pleasure out of just watching my face light up when he brought me home something special on a random day. He never waited for a holiday to do something special. From cooking me my favorite dish to buying me a fur coat and diamonds and every small and big thing in between, Patrice was incredibly generous to not only to me, but also to my daughter, our friends, and our family. He was so giving and he said that his generosity was based on selfishness. It simply fulfilled him to be able to make other people happy. I totally get that, and I reciprocated that to him in many areas of our life, including sex. Watching him experience all types of physical pleasure from another woman and seeing how his face would light up simply by pulling down her panties or touching her breasts was selfishly satisfying for me in the same way it was for him to see me open a box with a new diamond bracelet. He stated many times publically that engaging in threesomes made our love stronger, and people would just laugh. However, I am here to confirm, that statement is very true. But we did not get to that level overnight.

"We **(men)** *have 3 different things going on: our mind, our heart, and our dick. Women have one thing going on. It's all connected."* –Patrice O'Neal

Patrice and I had a very unique start to our relationship. As I described in an earlier chapter, we never actually "dated." We morphed into a loving relationship because he initially felt that I needed his friendship more than I needed him trying to coerce me into bed like he would do with every other woman he met. Besides, he had plenty of women he was juggling at the time, so it wasn't as if he needed me in the sex department from the beginning. So he chose to make me a student of his "karate class." Karate class was something that Patrice would refer to when he was speaking about his philosophies on relationships and the "training" a woman must go through to work with him in a relationship. Everyone starts out as a white belt, and everyone, with practice, consistency, and mental strength, has the opportunity to become a black belt—just like in a real life karate class. This was the analogy he used long before developing the analogy of the corporation. In this particular karate class, Patrice was the master teacher, and the women were the students. I was not a member of this karate class at first. As a platonic friend, I was only able to participate and learn through observation of him and all of his many, many chicks. Once he realized that I was in love with him after several months of me just observing, he felt that he should let me enter his class. How did he come to understand that I was in love with him? Well, he said it was the night that we "broke up as friends", which ultimately led to our first kiss.

The night we broke up as friends was so incredibly painful for me that I cried all the way home on the bus in front of many New York/New Jersey onlookers (who probably thought that someone close to me had died because of how distraught I was), with tears pouring down my face and blowing my nose in a flimsy tissue. When I finally got home, it got worse. I cried to my roommate and told her what happened, and she thought I was being ridiculous. I was basically an emotional wreck over my "friend" simply because he did not make a plate of food for me when I was at his house for dinner.

One day in the late afternoon, Patrice called me and said, *"Hey you broke-ass actress. I know you're hungry, living that starving artist life, so if you want to come over for dinner later, I am making lobster, rice, and broccoli for this chick that's coming over. You're more than welcome to come and eat, but then you got to leave because I am definitely trying to fuck her later."* Now, this was not at all a surprising phone call from Patrice. Remember, in the beginning of our relationship, we were just friends, so this type of call from Patrice was not rare. I, of course, accepted his invitation to dinner and took my half hungry, half quietly in love with him self over to his house to be a third wheel on his date. All was going well and normal when I got there. I had never met this woman, but Patrice had told me all about her. She was a teacher with big boobs and a pretty face, but no ass. That is exactly how he described her and that is exactly how she looked. Patrice was really into teachers, doctors, and lawyers at the time and did not mind that she had no ass. He said that a pretty face is absolutely necessary, but that he would take a woman shaped like anything. He particularly loved breaking down professional women, stripping away their corporate "I have a degree and I am a professional" attitude. He loved to prove that even the highest level of an accomplished woman was still just a "goofy girl with goofy girl thoughts." In addition, he loved professional women because he said they were usually the freakiest. But, getting back to the date, all was well until Patrice broke what I knew as our consistency, and I could not handle it. Usually, whenever I came over for dinner, Patrice would make my plate and bring it to me and then we would eat together. This time, he brought the teacher her plate and said to me, *"Von, you can make your own plate, you know where everything is,"* and began to eat and chat it up with the teacher while I went into the kitchen to fend for myself. I did not say anything at the time, but I am sure my attitude changed a bit. In addition to that little bit of hurt, Patrice added insult to injury when it was time for me to leave. Normally, he would either drive me home or get me a cab and talk to me on the phone until I got home. If for any reason he was not able to talk to me on the phone during the ride, he would insist that I called him once I got home so that he knew I got home safe. This time, when it was time for me to leave, he asked his roommate, who so happened to be leaving at the same time, if he would drop me off at home before heading into the city. His roommate said yes. I left with his roommate, and when I got home I did not bother calling because, not only did Patrice not ask me to, but also because I knew he was busy with the teacher. My feelings were so hurt and I had no way to communicate those feelings, not just to Patrice, but also to myself. At the time, my feelings were so mixed. I knew the situation bothered me, but I could not explain it. I was not trained at the time to understand entitlement, or consistency, or double standards, or the natural order of things, and Lord knows my communication skills we subpar. After that day, I became distant with Patrice for a short time and did not hang out or talk on the phone with him much. I bottled up those feelings, and Patrice never knew how that day affected me until several months later when I saw him again.

One night when I was out with my roommate who so happened to be dating a comedian friend of Patrice's, we bumped into Patrice in the village and he started talking to his friend. After a little while of chatting, his friend told Patrice he was going back to Jersey to spend the night at our place with my roommate, so Patrice, who lived in Jersey as well, offered us a ride home. On the surface, it appeared that he was giving us a ride only because his friend was coming over to spend the night with my roommate. However, in my mind, he really missed me and was happy to see me and would probably try and talk to me on the way home since I had been giving him the cold shoulder for so long. But of course, I got zero attention from Patrice on the ride home. He did not make any effort to talk to me

153

whatsoever. When we got to my apartment and everyone was wrapping up their conversations, I got out the car, slammed the door, and stormed away.

What puzzled me about Patrice is that he maintained the friend zone with me and always claimed that he was not interested in me. He maintained that story our entire lives together. He also claimed that in the beginning, he did not realize I was interested in him in a romantic way either, but I think he knew. Of course he knew. Patrice had a natural ability to see through people in seconds, so of course he should be able to tell that I was quietly in love with him. However, for whatever reason Patrice saw fit, he always chose to never admit that our beginning friendship was really the beginning of an unorthodox courtship that led into an unorthodox relationship. But at the time, I still had no way of communicating my feelings to Patrice. See, I was young and not trained in the manner of truth yet. I was beautiful and slightly arrogant in that I had never truly experienced rejection from a man like that before, so telling Patrice

that I was hurt seemed silly—yet inevitable.

Another week or so went by, and this time I was

hanging out in the village with a different female friend of

mine who lived in Brooklyn. She asked the guy she was

with to give us both a ride home, and although she lived

in Brooklyn and I lived in New Jersey, he agreed to take

us both home. Since we were near the Holland Tunnel,

the plan was to take me home to Jersey first, then take

her to Brooklyn. But, on our way to his car, we saw

Patrice sitting in his Lincoln Town Car outside of the

Comedy Cellar. I got butterflies in my stomach when he

looked at me and said *"Hey."* I had not seen him in what

felt like forever. Inside, I just wanted to run over to him

and touch and kiss his face, but of course I did not. There

was some small talk between the four of us as we were

walking past Patrice in his car that just basically informed

him of our plans to get home. We continued walking to

the other car. A minute or two after we got into my

friend's car, Patrice called me on my cell phone and asked

if I would rather he take me home. I was ecstatic. I

almost jumped out of the car and into Patrice's by doing

a ballerina twirl I was so happy! I was so happy because

in my mind, he was concerned about my safety. While he

knew the girl I was with, he was not familiar with the guy.

However, in Patrice's version of the story, he did not call

me because he was concerned. He would say he was

going to Jersey anyway and figured why not give me a

ride. Whichever way the story goes, I was already in a

moving vehicle by the time he called. I practically jumped

out of the car. "Pull over here!" I exclaimed. "Patrice is

going to pick me up on the corner so you guys can go

straight to Brooklyn." They were happy and so was I.

When I got in Patrice's car, it was awkward. I did

not know if I should smile or hit him, but I certainly did

not express my inner excitement outwardly. I wanted to,

but I did not know how. I only knew that I missed him. I

missed his face. I missed his smell. I missed him being my

friend. I missed his protection and concern. I missed his knowledge and words. I missed everything about him, but I still, at the time, had no idea how to express how I felt to him.

On our ride back to Jersey, Patrice began to explain to me how he was "righteous" in being my friend and not trying to fuck me like every other guy and how out of line I was to act jealous and hurt because of his actions the night the teacher was over. He explained to me that he was treating me like one of the guys, and how if I weren't a girl, that night would not have ended our friendship. He went on and on explaining to me all the "girl shit" I did and how I failed at being a friend back to him by letting feelings that I have for him make me lash out on him out of entitlement. He continued by pointing out my dishonesty in my actions; whatever feelings I had for him that left me hurt by that situation were all inner dialogue since I never told him my real feelings for him, which at this point were very obviously past friendship.

He said that I treated him how I would treat any man that was trying to sleep with me and that he did not deserve it because he was always genuine and never tried anything past what he promised me; he really wanted our friendship to teach me how to be better than what I was acting like when we first met. His words in this conversation were very well thought out, as usual. Mine were emotional. I could not fight his honesty, and besides, everything he was saying was right. He also smelled really good and I am sure he could see me "blinking slow" at him, as he would call it (blinking slow is when a person has a twinkle in their eyes for another person). So, in classic Patrice style, he suggested that in order for us to become friends again, we would have to kiss—not a big tongue kiss, but a nice kiss to make up for all the times he did not try to sleep with me. His rationale behind the kiss was that I at least owed him that for treating him like a guy who was trying to sleep with me when he was not doing anything in that realm. Now, to me (and probably to you as well), that sounds like some serious pimp style manipulation, but all I could think to myself at the time was, *YES! Finally! I knew it! He likes me! He wants to kiss me! Yes! Yes!*

Yes, in my mind, this was confirmation that he not only liked me, but he missed me just as much as I missed him. I could feel it. The energy in the car was intense as we pulled up to the front door of my apartment. I felt so nervous because I knew that it was time to kiss him once the car stopped, and he looked over at me as if to say, "So, give it up. I deserve at least a kiss so we can move on and be friends again without me resenting you." However, little did he know that in my mind, if I was going to go along with his pimp reasons as to why we should kiss, there was no way in hell I was going to do that and then just go back to friendship. I planned on joining his karate class for good. So, to make sure he felt the same (since of course I could not say it verbally), I said it with the kiss. Instead of giving him a peck on the lips like he requested, I gave him the tongue.

159

I let the kiss start off as a soft, small peck of the lips, but just when I felt like he was going to pull away, I grazed this bottom lip with my tongue. Naturally, he slightly opened his mouth and it became a full-blown, delicious, soft, wet kiss, in which he pulled me so close to him that it felt like I entered his body and our souls became one. It was great! In my mind, I had successfully and covertly entered into his karate class and was now in his circle of eligible women that he was dating that had the potential of getting a black belt and becoming Mrs. O'Neal. Approximately two or three weeks went past after our initial kiss and we are back to being buddies again with a similar routine as before, but now it was clear to him that I wanted to officially be in the running of somehow becoming Mrs. O'Neal someday, so for me, I felt we should take the next step.

"We have to be the best versions of ourselves to get a woman. All they have to do to get a man is flip their hair and wink." –Patrice O'Neal

In what stands to be one of the most hilarious moments of our entire relationship, Patrice loved to often describe what happened the night I invited him upstairs to my apartment for the first time as "pathetic." It was weird because we had never hung out in my place before. We had only been in his apartment or in public together. I knew once we got upstairs, I was going to try and seduce him, or actually, make myself available to be seduced by him. But to my surprise, once we got upstairs and in my room, he was just relaxing watching television, completely disregarding what I felt was the obvious reason for him being in my apartment. I got undressed after a while and put on less clothing. He still seemed not to notice. All I was thinking in my mind was, *What the hell? Did our kiss a few weeks ago mean nothing? Did he really just want that kiss to go back to just being friends? Am I not in the karate class now? Patrice is a smart guy, so he has to know why I asked him up here, right? Is he really serious about the whole "friends" thing?* With those thoughts in mind came the most comedic moment of our entire relationship, according to Patrice. In a moment of desperation, I got up to turn the television manually while bending over in front of the television as sexy as I could, exposing my nakedness under the t-shirt to him. I was not wearing any panties at the time, and I figured, *Ok, do you get it now?* The answer to that was yes. The next thing I remember after that moment is receiving the best oral sex that I had ever had in my life. He laid me down on the bed and pulled me to the edge while he got down on his knees on the floor and basically turned me completely out. He broke the picture frame that was behind him on the floor. I did not really care, but in classic Patrice style, he insisted on replacing it. That was it. No actual sex; just him giving me oral without wanting anything in return.

If Patrice were to tell the story, he would definitely maintain the fact that he did not know why I invited him up to my apartment. He would also say it was surprising and hilarious that the only way I could express that I wanted him was by bending over in front of the television. He said that that is the arrogance of women, that we can just expose ourselves to get sex from a man without having the pressure of verbally expressing anything. As always, he flipped it and said, *"What if I was to do that? No man can just bend over and show his balls to a woman and just get sex. Even the most attractive man with the largest penis has to have some type of charm and charisma to get sex."* He said that the arrogance of women suggests that we can turn men down sexually without any repercussions, but if he would have turned me down sexually after I basically threw myself at him, then I would have every right to say that he is probably gay.

Regardless of his observation of the situation, and no matter how many times he laughed at me for doing that, I expected him to know. I always expected him to just know everything. There is still a part of me that truly believes that he not only knew that night why I invited him up to my apartment, but he knew from the beginning

163

when I met him on the set of the 25th Hour that I was "blinking slow" at him. I tend to believe and understand that the biggest reason he denies ever liking me in the beginning or realizing that I liked him is because I would have expected him to because of my "pretty girl syndrome" and therefore would have been abusive and arrogant in the situation and we would not have lasted. He would never give me the satisfaction of him wanting me and relinquishing any power to me in those early stages. Him rejecting me ever so indirectly put me just where he would want any woman: it put me in a place in which I was forced to respect him, his time, and just his mere presence. I was forced to be humble. But all his actions from the beginning showed his affection for me. Innately, that was enough for me to believe he loved me from the beginning. Realistically, on the surface, it made me scared, insecure, and suspicious, all of which would play out in our near future. But at the time, if he let me know for one second that he had a place in his heart for me, I would have likely stomped all over it. He knew that.

I did not. I had so much to learn before I could handle a loving, respectful relationship, and I loved him even more for holding on to it. If Patrice had not seemingly rejected me in the beginning, we would have probably just been another typical one-night stand story. Not only did we not become a one-night stand story, we also did not have sex for about eight months after that first oral sex venture. We continued to have oral sex, but we did not have actual penetration for a long time, and that was Patrice's choice as well. He was a master at slowly easing you into different sexual experiences, and eventually we morphed into not only a sexual relationship, but also a real relationship filled with commitment and threesomes.

After a few years, Patrice and I were finally together, and all of the women in his karate class were gone, but his desire for other women was not gone. We always maintained the same open communication with each other, even after our friendship grew into commitment to one another. Patrice had me so used to

165

learning and accepting his "man truth" that I was not surprised or hurt by him admitting that yes, he loved me, but his nature still prevailed. He loved the smell, taste, and feel of "new pussy" and I loved the intense feeling of pleasuring my man (and the freakiness of engaging in taboo sexual activities).

What people have to understand is that building trust takes time. That is the reality that most women do not want to let marinate and develop. We want trust as soon as we walk in the door of a new relationship. In fact, we start out on a bad foot with men usually because we come in defensive with all types of built up "I don't trust him" walls protecting us from the lies he has not even told to us yet. What Patrice wanted to do with all women was give us different options on how to think in general, but especially in this area of trust. *"Trust is consistency over time"* he would say all the time. He would go deeper and say to me *"trust is a routine."* So what does that mean exactly? Well, first and foremost, it means you need time with a person to build a routine and to see what their consistency is, not only with you, but also in their life in general. Humans in general, but especially men, are creatures of habit, and you need time to understand what is important to your partner and what their routines are.

"I trust people to do exactly what they are going to do" –Patrice O'Neal

The word trust has almost become synonymous with mistrust. The word itself sounds somewhat scary and negative even when you are telling someone you trust him or her. What you are saying underneath that statement is really, "I am scared. Please do not hurt me and prove my suspicions to be correct." But if you examine the routine you have built with this person, then you can logically see if you are being paranoid or not. If you have not spent enough time with this person to understand their routine and patterns with you, then you are out of line, and you certainly have no right to be territorial. You are way ahead of yourself and yes, he or she is probably dating and/or sleeping with someone else. As discussed, when you meet someone, nine times out of ten, yes, they have other people in their life working towards the same spot you want. If you find that man attractive and appealing, then go ahead and assume that many other women of your stature, higher and lower, all feel similar towards him as well. Always remember, men are not in the business of turning women down. They are in the mindset of the old school saying, "Collect, collect, collect, select." If you think you are going to just burst open the door of his life day one and demand his full, undivided attention and time, then think again. It takes time, and unfortunately for us ladies, with a lot of men, the building process takes longer than what we have patience for, especially if we let our insecure suspicious minds drive our actions.

With Patrice, I had already spent a couple of years getting to know many different sides of him and his routines and desires, so when we finally decided to start building something together, whenever my suspicious, jealous mind would start wondering, he would remind me to "stay surface happy." In other words, in the early stages of a relationship, its best to not dig too deep because you are going to find something that will bring the development of your one-on-one relationship with him to a stop. Unless that is what you want, do not dig. Stay on the surface and build confidence in the relationship through time and consistency. Patrice wanted me to stay strong and rise above any childish feelings I had with jealously, mistrust, entitlement, and insecurity; all of which were what he felt was the root of possessiveness. He felt that if he could help me rise above all of those things, then he could show me what a wonderful relationship built of desire could be with another person, as opposed to most people's miserable relationships that start out with desire, then shift into obligation and possessiveness.

Patrice felt like most women in relationships get to that point where they claim ownership over their man and begin to dictate his every move, not because it is good for him, but because it is good for their own insecurity. He said that he would never give enough power to any woman to make him feel like he had to lie to her for any reason. If I were to ask, Patrice, "Do you have other women in your life?" during the early stages of our relationship when he did, he would have absolutely have said *"Yes, feel better now pumpkin?"* Of course that would not make me feel better, so I knew not to ask and to stay in the matrix. However, I did not always succeed.

One time in our early stages, Patrice left his cell phone in the car with me while he went into the Comedy Cellar to talk to one of his friends for a moment. So in true girl fashion, I started to dig and search through his phone, reading all of his text messages. To my surprise, not only was Patrice talking to other women, but he was also saying the exact same things to them that he was saying to me. See, at the time, I thought all the karate class talk and information he was giving was special and unique to me, but it certainly was not. When Patrice got back in the car and looked at my face, he immediately knew something was wrong. He looked over at me and said, "What's wrong pumpkin?" I, with a tear falling down my face said, "I looked through your phone."

To my surprise, I was not scolded or yelled at in any way for my disrespectful snooping. Patrice actually took a very gentle, understanding approach and said, *"Do you feel better now?"* I looked up at him with confusion on my face as if to say, *of course not, don't you see I am crying!* But before I could say a word, he began to explain. He said to me that I should have stayed in the matrix of just what goes on between the two of us. When I decided to snoop in his phone, I took the pill that opened me up to a reality that I was not ready for, but since I was now exposed, he would help talk me through it logically. This was the first time I remember ever feeling hurt and relieved at the

171

same time. Patrice was telling me the absolute, explicit truth—something I had never gotten from a man before. I expected him to yell and argue with me. I was expecting him to lie and deny the women in his phone. I thought that I was about to have to break up with him, but no, he helped me understand that yes, he does talk to other women and say the same things because we, at that particular time, were all on the same level in his life. We were all on the same level in his karate class. At that point in our relationship, I had not grown into a fully committed relationship with him yet, so he admitted that he was still seeing a couple of the women that he was dating before we even met. He also pointed out to me that I already knew about some of those women when he and I were just friends, but now that I was officially in the karate class, I felt entitled and territorial. He also told me something that I will never forget that I thought was so honest and amazing. When I asked about why he said the same thing to all of us and explained to him that that was what hurt the most, he said there were two reasons: one was that we were all on the same level, and two, men say

the same things to women that are all on the same level

so that they do not have to remember who they said what

to. Everyone gets the same information, and what she

does with it will either promote her or get her released

from the class. I felt like Patrice had just given me a

profound secret that only men knew, and although I was

upset, it made sense, and I was utterly relieved that he

told me the truth. I truly felt closer to him in that I was

able to take that truth, understand it, deal with it, and

one-hundred percent know where I stood with him,

always, since he was willing to be honest and clear up my

confusion. The truth is never confusing, and it is

something that I always wanted. This painful dose of

truth was just the medicine I needed. Eventually, all of

these women were released because, unlike me, I was

happy to be fed the truth, even if it hurt. Eventually, it

was just my man and I, a threesome here and there, and

no need for the matrix. I spent a lot of time in the early

part of our relationship working through some hardcore

truth. But the truth, as they say, will set you free. What I want to stress is that getting to the point of being in a successful monogamous relationship with Patrice was a transitional process. It did not just happen.

No matter how far you come in a relationship, as a woman, you will always have to fight your natural feelings of jealousy, but know how to overcome and control your actions realistically. If you do not want to leave him, do not look for any reason to leave him. If you find something, you will leave. But if you want to leave, just leave. Why make it his fault? If you do not find anything, you just violated his trust and space and now there is just cause for him to leave you. So ultimately, if you are happy, just be happy, stay in the matrix, and keep building. A man's desire for "new pussy" is just a physical obstacle to get over like a woman's menstrual cycle. Men do not have sex attached to their hearts and emotions like women do. I especially learned that doing threesomes and dealing with women. I understand how men can have sex with us and not even know our last names. In fact, I can't even tell you the first or last names of most of the women we were with. I honestly only remember one name, and that is because I knew her for many years from bartending in the theatre district. If I did not know her prior, I would not remember her either. That is just the way it is. We are physical, visual objects to men, and we have to work our way up to being loved and cared for in a relationship. So I get it. A man can be happy with his wife at home and still want "new pussy." If a happy man still cheats on his woman, it is physical, and usually does not have much to do with his wife. A happy woman cheating on her husband does not exit. A man can get his rocks off with a random chick and not look at his wife or treat his wife any different. A woman who cheats, because we are not just visual creatures, have to like something else about a man, his swag, his pockets, his charm, then the added bonus is his sexy body, juicy lips, and big penis. If a fine man is corny in our eyes, we look at his fineness as a waste. Men do not generally care

175

about a woman's accomplishments or personality deeply at first. *"Halle Barry's pussy is the same as the bitch who works at McDonalds,"* Patrice would say. *"Men start from the bottom up. We start from pussy, then work our way up to 'Can you read?'"* Women are the opposite.

With that being said, since women have to like something other than a man's physicality, it is hard to disconnect our emotions because our interest in a man start with an attachment to our emotions. If a woman is cheating, then whatever it is that she likes about the other man will in turn be against her husband because it is probably something he lacks. For instance, if the other man smells real good and calls you beautiful, takes you out to nice dinners, makes you laugh, shows you a good time, and the sex is great, you will look at your husband for all the things that he is not doing or cannot do that the other man is doing. You will naturally lose respect for your husband and his manhood and begin treating him like less than your husband. You will resent him for things unbeknownst to him. So, from Patrice's perspective, if a man cheats, the relationship can stay intact (if the woman stays in the matrix) because it would purely be physical and would not change his feelings or actions towards his woman; their relationship can survive. If a woman cheats, then the relationship is over. As mentioned earlier when discussing double standards, attention is to a woman, what pussy is to a man. The only difference is the attachment.

In our case, we found a connected love and increased happiness in supplying each other's needs sexually on very high levels of intimacy, and eventually he did not need any other woman in his life except me and our occasional threesomes. As he would say, *"My woman in my life is worth at least five or six bitches."* That type of pure honesty between two people is the pathway to true friendship filled with love and happiness.

Chapter 7

Love & Happiness

"I had to figure out a way to make myself happy, and that's not to lie."

— Patrice O'Neal

LOVE & HAPPINESS

While I am sure all women, including me, would like to fantasize that there is a perfect man out their looking for you to call you his rib, we must take a more realistic approach to understanding what a Prince Charming really is in the pursuit of love and happiness. First, let us women get rid of the notion that some perfectly chiseled dude will ride in on a white horse and take us off into the sunset to awaken in the morning in a beautiful house with a white picket fence and 2.5 kids. Personally, horses make me itch, and most of the contemporary mansions that I imagine living in do not have any type of picket fence around it messing up the décor. In other words, that is old school thinking. It is something out of a fairy tale that we used to believe back when we thought Santa Claus, the Easter Bunny and the Tooth Fairy were real. However, as a woman, I understand why we hold on to our childhood princess dreams. It feels good. It is painful to find out that many of our male counterparts have a very different fantasy, and it usually involves having several princesses in his castle to share in his love, protection, home, and of course, his body. The problem arises when we look at our childish fantasy as valid and a man's childish fantasy as just that, childish. Let's face it, we all want and desire what we want, although when we mature as adults, we still want to somehow obtain a realistic version of our childhood dreams and the husband and/or wife that we always imagined.

Love and happiness is possible, if you first start believing that it is and stop daydreaming about unrealistic fantasies. The truth about being happy is that there is no happiness without peace. Peace is happiness. You have to make peace with the fact that relationships are imperfect, much like all aspects of life. It is a constant circle of ups and downs filled with good days and bad days that are filled with good decisions and bad decisions. At some point in life, people make the statement, "I am only human" to refer to their own faults and excuse themselves from their imperfections and mistakes. Many of us have even found ourselves making a similar statement for friends, saying, "You're only human," to make them feel better during a hard time or disappointment from a mistake in their life. But for some reason, we have a difficult time excusing our partners. We insist on having some type of perfect relationship in a world that we all agree is imperfect. That is not a rational thought—that is a fantasy. If we can find some acceptance and empathy for ourselves as well as our partners, things may go a bit smoother. Most importantly, stop analyzing and judging your partner's every move in an attempt to change them into what you want them to be as opposed to accepting them and compromising, or moving on to your true imperfect match.

Before I met Patrice, I wrote down on a piece of paper exactly what type of man I wanted, and when Patrice showed up in my life, he was almost everything on the list. As a spiritual person who believes in the law of attraction, I was not surprised that the number one thing on my list was exactly the number one thing that Patrice was: honest. It was at the top of my list of what I needed in a man, and I felt like if I could find that in a man, everything else would just be a bonus. But, like they say, be careful what you wish for because you just might get it. Just because we want something in life does not mean it will be easy to get or maintain. My young naïve self had no idea what real honesty looked like and what it would take to endure. I, like many women, thought I could take man truth; eventually I became a pro at it, but it wasn't easy. Much like a career or any goal, there will be challenges and growth pains, and only the strong survive. There are many rewards in crossing the finish line into happiness and peace. But you must first realize that there is no real finish line. Much like in a career, what appears to be a finish line is something that just keeps morphing into another level and higher goal to reach. We have all heard the term "growing apart," and realistically that is what happens with many couples. Admittedly, it is rare that two people find each other and grow together in love with each other and in themselves. I was blessed and will never take for granted the magical experience I had with Patrice and I do hope to find magic again. But, I know going into any new relationship will take time. Whatever level you are at you should try your best to just enjoy the journey with your partner and not live in misery while making another person's life miserable as well. It is not worth it for either of you, and if such is the case, you should move on to find someone more compatible. You will not get any of the days of your life back, so why waste time being and creating unhappy relationships. I know that is easier said than done, but the idea behind writing this book is to inspire you to at least try. Moreover, if you find yourself in a pattern of misery, please take an honest look at yourself and how you are contributing to what is going wrong in the relationships that do not work out. It will be worth it in the end to be honest with yourself and your partner. It is not *always* the other person's fault, and men are not always wrong.

Finding peace, love, and happiness is priceless; after all, I must reiterate: you will not get any of your days back. It is only fair to try and make sure every day that your life is pleasurable not only for yourself, but for the people that you love so that there are no regrets; the only compromises you should make are ones that you can truthfully, honestly live with.

I was fortunate enough to be able to live a realistic lifestyle of love with my Prince Charming, but it came at a price. The price was compromise. People mistake compromise with suppression. Patrice and I certainly found a way to accommodate each other's needs through honesty without hurting one another, and that is the key to happiness. Everyone wants to feel genuine love. I can count on one hand in ten years how many times Patrice actually told me he loved me. But the actions in which he showed me how much he loved me were countless and never ending. He said to me one day when I complained about not hearing the words I love you often enough, *"You have had many guys in your life tell you that they love you, but you still have no clue what love is. Do you want me to say I love you, or show you what love really is? Pick one."* I picked show me. He was right. I had no clue what love was, nor did I know what true happiness was in a relationship. Patrice refused to live by rules and standards. He would randomly buy me gifts and tell me that I never have to worry about holidays because it is always my birthday. It was always Valentine's Day and Christmas, and he said if I had to wait for any particular holiday for someone to express sharing and giving, then it's probably not genuine. He insisted on sharing out of desire, not out of rules or obligation.

Patrice believed that the key to a successful relationship lied within the man, the king of the castle. *"Happiness trickles down from the King,"* he would say to me. *"Take care of the King, and the Queen will be alright."* He believed that women were designed to be "miserable." He felt that it was in our DNA to spoil fun, worry, love and care for kids overbearingly, and be emotional about everything. *"A man's love is practical,"* he would say, while *"a woman's love is internal."* Using ejaculation and pregnancy as an example, Patrice would illustrate the reason why it is easier for a man to not be around and raise a kid he fathered while woman are mostly instantly attached. *"A man can cum inside of you, or he can cum on a sock. Women, everything that happens to them, even a sexual climax, are all internal."*

The point he was getting to was that because of a woman's nature and genetic makeup, happiness could only trickle down from the King. You have to take care of the King because if the King is happy, he will create a happy home for his Queen to be miserable in. *"Complete happiness does not exist in women. They will always find something wrong. They have no peace. They always want more."*

As I mature, I do not know that I fully agree with the idea that women are completely and utterly insatiable

186

and will always seek more once given their needs and wants. Even during the latter part of our relationship, I started to notice how my desires would always naturally increase as the relationship progressed, but at the same time, I would find patience to deal with that. I noticed how happy I was becoming with just being grateful for what I had and trusted that things would naturally progress. Since Patrice's life, and therefore our relationship, was cut short, our experiences together never got to mature past where we were and we never got to truly see what we would have matured into together once we were officially married. Overall, I truly believe that love and respect are the same thing. You cannot convince me that you love me if you do not respect me and vice versa. Patrice gave me and taught me not only how to receive love and respect from him, but how to give it as well. He taught me how to get what I want from a man without force. He taught me how to be a desirable woman above my physicality. He taught me how to get and maintain his continued desire to love and respect me as his woman—his queen. I cannot stress enough how much happier you can be as a woman if you receive a man's love and respect without force or ultimatums. It may take longer than jumping the broom of lies, but it certainly is worth the wait and sacrifice. However, as a man, if you know that your woman has done due diligence in the relationship and is patiently awaiting the deserved promotion, it is your responsibility to recognize when the time is right to move into the next level, because if you wait too long, it can prove to be detrimental.

Chapter 8

For Men's Eyes Only

"I realized that pimps aren't magical. They're just men who take advantage of the women who love them."

— *Patrice O'Neal*

FOR MEN'S EYES ONLY

In the prior chapter when I was discussing my relationship with Marlow, I mentioned that my relationship with him was the only relationship that I ever had that did not leave me with any baggage, and yes, if I am being completely honest, that includes my relationship with Patrice. While I credit Patrice for helping me to become the woman that I am today on so many levels, teaching me how to be a better mother, wife, friend, and so much more, I was still left with an enormous amount of baggage when he died because we were not legally married. On top of losing my best friend and lover, I also lost my home and many possessions attached to precious memories. Part of the mourning process when you lose someone is taking the time to go through things and deciding what to keep and what to let go of, but I was not able to do that because Patrice and I were not legally married. Patrice died approximately one month prior to our wedding date, and we both suffered because of it. He suffered in the hospital leading up to his death, and I not only suffered during that time in the hospital with him, but I suffered thereafter in life.

We were together for ten years, and our lifestyle suggested that we were married at least five years into our relationship. In fact, there were many people that did not know that we were not legally married because he always introduced me as his wife after a certain point in our relationship. We never felt it was necessary to rush to get married; after all, what does a piece of paper from the government have to do with proving our love? Well, as we both found out the hard way when Patrice had the stroke that ultimately took his life, being legally married has everything to do your love for one another. It puts the person that you are the closest to and most intimate with in control of your destiny. When Patrice first had the stroke, I was not able to sign certain papers that may have helped him suffer less. I was not able to permit visitors, and many of his close friends did not get to see him before he died. There are some people that believe that it was I who would not allow them to visit Patrice in the hospital, but that just proves right there how little people know about rules and power. I was not the one with the power in the hospital to decide who would be allowed to see Patrice. I was not even able to reject the people that were being allowed to visit Patrice that I knew he would not want there at all—especially in place of his close friends. I was not even in control of making sure Patrice's final wishes were met. Patrice did not want a funeral or a traditional burial. He wanted to be cremated and for me to spread his ashes on top of Corcovado Mountain in Rio de Janeiro, Brazil, where we once visited together. I had no power to ensure his wishes were met. I did my best, but the truth is, all I could do was make suggestions and watch everything unfold from the sidelines. Of course I knew exactly what Patrice wanted me to do in the event that he would ever be unable to make decisions for himself. We talked about it when we were in Brazil several years prior to his death and several times throughout the year that he died. However, since we were not married, I had no power and there was not much I could do about anything. All I really could do was make suggestions, and hope for the best.

I remember the summer before he died when we were discussing life and what to do in the event that something happened to one another, telling Patrice that we had to set a date to get married because if anything ever happened to him and I was not able to do all these things that he was telling me I should do, then it would be his fault. He decided during this discussion that we would get married before the end of the year, and we both agreed that it would be nice to get married in Hawaii, where we were planning to go for Christmas vacation. We set that as a tentative date. We never made it to that date. He died November 29, 2011.

The fall of 2011 was the most I had ever seen Patrice work the entire time we were together. He was finishing up a feature film called *Nature Calls*, and while in the last days of shooting the film in New York, he had to fly to LA to make what became his final television appearance on the highly rated Comedy Central Roast of Charlie Sheen. When he got back from the roast, he had to complete the last day of shooting for *Nature Calls* and then perform at several comedy shows, including his final headlining gig at Caroline's On Broadway. Two weeks after his final stand-up performance at Caroline's, he was scheduled to fly back to California to meet with FX executives for his new television show. According to Patrice, FX had said that they wanted him to be the "Black Louie CK of the network" and that he had an advanced green light on whatever he wanted to do. The script that he wanted to present for that show was loosely based on the moment I told Patrice I used to date Marlow.

In 2007, I told Patrice about my relationship with Marlow when he said that he had to fly to Los Angeles to audition for a new film anticipated to be another blockbuster comedy hit because it was starring Marlow and one of the Cosby kids. This moment in time proved to be the second most hilarious moment of my relationship with Patrice. I told Patrice that out of respect I should let him know that I used to deal with Marlow. Patrice called me goofy and said he could have gone his whole life not knowing that I was ever with him. As a woman, my intention and point of view were completely opposite his. I told Patrice that out of respect, I would always tell him about everyone I ever was with if I found out they were friends or worked together or would be associated with each other in any close capacity. I felt that if I did not tell him and he found out somehow, I would then look like I was trying to hide something. Patrice's response to that was asking me how I thought he would have ever found out. He said, *"Marlow would never just walk up to me and say, 'Ay yo man, I popped ya girl.'"* I one-hundred percent agreed with Patrice in that, no, Marlow would never do that. But, that did not change my stance. I still felt like it would be disrespectful to my man to be in a room with another man with a secret, so I told him. I still feel that I did the right thing by telling Patrice about Marlow. Patrice on the other hand did what he always does. He stood his ground and he made fun of the situation. He said to me, *"Damn bitch, you fucked so many comedians, your pussy should have better timing."* We both laughed hysterically and moved on. All was well, and as far as I knew, my past did not bother him at all. He did not get the part in Marlow's new movie, and to be honest, I did not even ask about how the audition went when he was in California. We never talked about my relationship with Marlow again, but when we began working on the treatment for his new FX pilot several years later in 2011, certain elements from that day were evident. The final script to be presented to FX was not only inspired by the day I told Patrice about Marlow, but it also revealed to me that maybe it did bother him a bit more than what he was willing to share directly. As an artist and writer myself, I let go of directly discussing it and went along with how he wanted to deal with it, and that was artistically. If it bothered him enough to want to talk about it, we would have. As a woman, I always took Patrice's lead. I felt that if I would have pressed the issue and started digging, it would have probably started an unnecessary quarrel. Besides, why bother? The fact that I had revealed that information to Patrice did not change our relationship one bit. It just became another comedy bit in our life and Patrice's material, as did just about everything in our life. Our life was handled with laughter in good times and bad. This particular time was no exception. It was just a moment in our relationship that became a script. Patrice and his writing partner, Gino Tomac, completed the final script. It was hilarious, and Patrice was very confident that it would make a great pilot episode. That was the best part about being in a relationship with Patrice. No matter what the situation was, I never felt judged. I never felt like anything I ever told him would be a deal breaker. I knew he loved me unconditionally, and I cannot stress to you how relieving and fulfilling it is to be with someone who accepts you,

197

your past, and all of your flaws, both physically and mentally. I was confident that nothing could tear us apart—nothing of course, except death.

To recapitulate, during the months leading up to October 2011 when Patrice had his stroke, he had been working more than I had ever seen in the ten years I had known him. The film *Nature Calls* was being shot in New York. The Charlie Sheen roast was being shot in Los Angeles. Patrice had to fly out to do the Charlie Sheen Roast over the weekend and make it back to New York by Monday for the final shot of the movie. I had never seen Patrice so nervous and worried about doing a show like he was about doing the Charlie Sheen Roast. He kept saying that if his part was not edited the right way, it could set him back seven years in his career, and he just did not have the time or energy left in him to climb out of a setback. When the Charlie Sheen Roast aired, I literally had to talk him through the entire show. This was something that I had never had to do before in the entire ten years we were together. He was willing to be vulnerable in front of me, and in some ways, afraid. He allowed me to be his strength. After he saw that it was edited in such a way that did not make him look like more of an ass than he would find acceptable for himself, he was fine. He moved on and proceeded to headline at Caroline's, work on the FX script, finalized with me his plans for his first comedy album that he had recorded at the DC Improv, and of course, our wedding plans. Patrice told me that he would have a two-week break after his last show at Caroline's before he had to go back to Los Angeles to meet with the FX executives about his new television show. During that two-week break is when he planned to sit down with me and solidify everything necessary in closing the date for our Hawaiian vacation and wedding date. We also were going to both complete our last will and testament, as well as clear up the lapse in his health insurance. On October 19, 2011, two days into that two-week break period, Patrice had a stroke.

The day Patrice had the stroke was a typical day for us. I had worked a late shift at the bar where I had been working for seven years, and we had talked several times throughout the day on the phone as normal. He wanted me to help him organize all of his video footage on the various video cameras he had laying around the house, and we were discussing doing that the next day. He wanted to get more organized and he was also contemplating how to fit his new podcast equipment on his desk. He was being encouraged to do a weekly podcast by many of his comedian friends and fans and we were attempting to figure out how to fit it into his schedule. We last spoke around 10pm, and it appeared that he was done for the night and would probably go to bed early. Several hours later, he called me and said that he thought he was having a stroke. I asked him why he thought that, and he said that he could not move his legs. He said that he was stuck in the chair at his desk. He said that when he woke up to go to the bathroom, one of his legs was numb, so he dragged himself from the bed to the desk area where his cell phone was so he could call me. By the time he was able to dial my number, both legs went numb, and he was stranded in the chair. I stayed very calm and told him that I was on my way to the house and would call 911. Patrice's normally strong voice was very low and quiet, though coherent. When I called 911, I told them that he was unable to walk and he was on the second floor of our condo. I asked them to be sure to send very strong men to get him down the stairs. I was very specific, telling them that he was 6'5" and 350 lbs. I drove as fast as I could, running every red light, anxiously trying to get to the house. After all, even if the paramedics got there before me, there was no way for them to get in the house because Patrice could not get out of the chair and I was the only other person with a key. By the grace of God, I arrived at the house at the same time as the paramedics, only to find that they had sent two people to help aide Patrice—and one was a woman.

When I saw Patrice sitting in the chair, he seemed to be coherent but out of it at the same time. His voice was still very quiet and low, and he was speaking very slowly. For the first time in the ten years I knew him, I saw him cry. I wiped the tear from his eye, kissed him several times on his forehead where he would always kiss me, and told him not to worry—that it would be just like it was when he went into the hospital a few years ago in 2005 for his high blood pressure. Trying to be strong and emulate a nonchalant attitude about the situation to lessen his worry like he did for me when I was about to have surgery, I told him that we would probably only be in the hospital for a few days. I assured him that I had grabbed all of his things from his closet that I was supposed to put in the bag so he would have everything he needed while in the hospital. I grabbed two black t-shirts, a pair of jeans, his slippers, his phone, and his iPad. While I was trying to be positive, strong, optimistic, and supportive, I think that Patrice knew he was nearing the end.

202

The emergency room was packed with people, and quite frankly, dirty. The room where they placed Patrice had blood smeared on the floor and dirty towels on the counter. All I could think of was getting him out of there. The doctors and nurses kept putting me off, telling me to stay calm and wait for Patrice to be sent to x-rays for a CT scan. The CT scan results would determine if they could move him to another hospital or not. As we were waiting, Patrice started to loose mobility in his arms. As the nurses were coming in to have paperwork signed, he was not able to do it, so he told the nurse to let me sign everything. She looked at me and asked, "Are you his wife?" I said, "Yes." He looked up and said, *"Yes, that is my wife."* She said, "Are you legally married?" We both answered no, and she walked out of the room, saying that if we were not legally married, then I would not be permitted to sign any paperwork. Patrice looked up at me silently as if to say he was sorry. I just walked over to the bed and sat close to him, wiping his sweat from his head, reassuring him that he would be ok and not to worry—that I would take care of everything for him in whatever way possible. Shortly thereafter, Patrice started swinging the one arm that he still had mobility in aimlessly in the air and said to me, *"Help me, I can't see."* I ran to get the doctor, and from that point, Patrice was in a coma. Those would be his last words he would ever speak.

Shortly thereafter, they confirmed the results of the CT scan. Patrice was indeed having a stroke and had a very large blood clot that needed removed. They approved a transfer to Englewood Hospital. Englewood Hospital is one of the best hospitals in the country, where they had the top surgeons in the nation that could do an emergency surgical procedure to remove the blood clot that caused the stroke and possibly save his life. However, the doctor suggested that I call his next of kin while waiting for the transfer paramedics because it did not look promising. I was afraid to call his mother at first because Patrice was very protective of her and was always concerned about her health. He never wanted to alarm or worry her and refused to allow me to contact her initially. In any case, dealing with his health, he always wanted to tell his mom himself after he found that everything was ok. But Patrice was now unconscious and for the first time in our relationship I had to make an incredibly difficult decision on his behalf without him. I had to decide whether or not to go against Patrice's rule and call his mom. This was the first of many future moments in which I felt like I had to now step into a position of power that Patrice always held as the man, and solely take full responsibility of making life-changing decisions. I took a deep breath, and I sat outside of his room and called his mother. I made sure to not call her while in the room with Patrice because the doctors told me that although he was not able to speak, he could possible still hear everything that was going on and to not verbalize anything around him that may be stressful to him. She of course was distraught and made immediate plans to come from Boston. The doctors told me that I may not be able to ride in the ambulance with Patrice during the hospital transfer, so I should call someone who could drive me to the hospital behind the ambulance just in case. As it was explained to me, if I were his wife, riding with him in the ambulance would not be in question.

When the paramedics arrived to take Patrice to Englewood Hospital, one of them recognized Patrice and said to me, "Don't worry Von, we will take good care of Patrice. I am a big fan of his. You can ride in the ambulance with us." He was very kind and got us to Englewood Hospital quickly and we went directly to the surgical team that was awaiting Patrice's arrival. While Patrice was in surgery, and his mom was on her way from Boston, some of Patrice's closest friends arrived at the hospital: Colin Quinn, Jim Norton, Keith Robinson, Robert Kelly, Rich Vos, and Wil Sylvince were all there. By the time Patrice got out of surgery, his mom had arrived. The doctors said the surgery was successful in removing the blood clot, but that it would take a couple of days to see how his body would respond. The doctor showed me a picture of the blood clot he removed. It was huge, and according to the doctor, it struck the most vulnerable part of a person's body; it struck his brain stem.

Keith was the first person to come into the room with Patrice's mom and me to see Patrice; then it was decided that no one else could come in after that because it may be too stressful for Patrice at first. Visitation would be granted later when he was feeling better and possibly conscious again, which of course never happened. It was not until the very last days of his life that very select people were allowed to come, but by then it was a little too late and many close friends did not get to say their goodbyes. Again, I did my best, but all I could do was make suggestions and watch from the sidelines. Englewood hospital was very gracious during his stay in the intensive care unit and gave Patrice's mom and me a room to sleep in. We literally lived in the hospital the entire time Patrice was there. Unfortunately, after the first few days, Patrice's health declined, and it was not promising that he would recover. Many doctors said that he had less than a 10 percent chance of recovering, and that number declined to less than 1 percent in just one week. It was determined that Patrice would be in a vegetative state for the rest of his life, and we were left with the decision of leaving him on the machine in a coma, or letting him go. Actually, the decision was ultimately not mine because of course I had no power, but I knew what Patrice would want, and I was verbally honest about it to everyone. Patrice and I had discussed it many times in the past; recently, when we were discussing getting married and doing our last will and testament, he said, *"You better let me go. You better not leave me all balled up in a bed not able to talk."* I knew what needed to be done, but I could not see it through for Patrice. While I was involved in the decision making process, I had no actual power, so the process and suffering lasted much longer than what it probably should have. During that time, I tried to do my best to make Patrice comfortable.

Because of my prior relationship with Marlow and the information he shared with me about his experiences while he was in a comatose state after having a stroke, I really believed that Patrice could hear me reading to him and playing his music in his ears every day. I knew Patrice's daily routine, and I woke up every day to take his mind through it, hoping that it was bringing him some type of comfort in his last days. I would read MediaTakeOut.com, TMZ, and watch Maury Povich with him. The NBA was in a lockout at the time, so I would keep him updated with the happenings in the NBA world. I would rub his feet and exercise his arms and legs for him to keep his blood flowing, but it was inevitable; Patrice was going to die, and everyone's life would be changed forever. I started playing one of his favorite songs to him more often in a last attempt to inspire Patrice to open his eyes and come back to us, and that song was Carly Simone's "No One Does It Better." The reason I chose that one in particular is because Patrice told me that in his early days of comedy when he used to drive back and forth from Boston, the lyrics of this song made him realize who he was. He said he played this song over and over, singing it to himself for the entire four-hour drive. The epiphany he had listening to this song was that he was a great comedian, that he was a high-level thinker, that he was funny, and, most importantly, that no one could do what he does better. He said he realized in his mind and felt in his heart at that moment that comedy needed him. I was hoping by playing that song in his ears over and over, maybe it was possible he would hear our cries for him not to leave us just yet in a different way. I was hopeful that hearing those lyrics he once sang to himself would spark an emotion and he would remember how important he was to all of us and how much we needed him in our lives, and in the world. Undoubtedly it was true; no one does it better than Patrice. Regardless of all of our efforts, the truth we had to face was that his time here on Earth had expired, and now we were all on our own.

"Death is hard on the living." –Patrice O'Neal

Like I said, I knew Patrice did not want a funeral, but I had no power to control that. I later realized that he would probably have been ok with the funeral, especially for his mother's sake. I realized that funerals are not for the dead. Funerals are for the living. The funeral was a beautiful ceremony and proved to be exactly as I would imagine Patrice would approve—if he would approve at all. His close friends including Jim Norton, Rich Vos, Wil Silvince, Robert Kelly, Colin Quinn, Kevin Hart, and my daughter all spoke at the funeral. The repast was held at Caroline's on Broadway. I wore a white dress to the funeral. It was the dress I had planned on wearing when we got married in Hawaii. Patrice experienced in death the consequences of us not being legally married, and in the days, weeks, months, and years ahead, I would experience, the hard way, what happens in life to couples that are not married. I cannot stress enough to the men reading this book how important it is to take that final step in your relationship sooner than later, especially if you have a good woman that is trying her best to learn your language and create a happy home and relationship. Remember, the king upgrades the queen. If a man asks a woman to marry her, it is an upgrade. If a woman asks a man to marry her, it is an ultimatum.

"Do right by others without doing wrong by yourself."

—Patrice O'Neal

In conclusion, if you love a woman, it is your responsibility not to take advantage of her love. Patrice went through a phase in his life in which he watched tons of documentaries and YouTube video footage of real life pimps and hookers. He was fascinated by their dynamic. He could not imagine what a man could possibly say to a woman that would inspire her to sell her body and give him the money. Ultimately he learned that in general the pimps were simply taking advantage of the women who loved them. In many instances, these women counted on their man for protection and direction, and the pimps basically encouraged them in the wrong direction. Such may be the case in your relationship. Take the steps to take care of your woman, as you know she is intending to also take care of you. Do not be the type of man that has a woman willing to do things, such as engage in threesomes for instance, but still cheat on her. If having a woman that is in tune with your desires and is down to participate in those desires is not enough to accommodate you, then that is a sure sign that you are not ready to be in a relationship. You should be single. At the end of the day, honesty prevails, and doing *"right by others without doing wrong by yourself"* will open the doors of success in many areas of your life and relationships. Patrice gave me life-changing truth that enabled me to speak fluent Patrice and man. Although we did not make it to our wedding date and beyond, I have hope that you can make it to yours by finding your truth and applying whatever you have learned through my story. I wish you a long life of blessings with your partner. With love, respect, and honor for one another, and without taking one moment of each other's time or friendship for granted, hopefully you will experience a similar joy in your relationships that I shared with Patrice. For the short time that God shared him with me on Earth, I was given life-changing truth that made me the woman I am today. The power of the growth I experienced in my life with Patrice enabled me to survive his death and step into a new dimension in which his philosophies will be carried on in ways neither of us could have ever foreseen. I have been more than proud and honored to share him and our truth with you, respectfully and lovingly.

Until we meet again, I love you Patrice, and I hope that you are proud.

With Love,

Von

NEW BEGINNINGS

"I only credit myself for listening and applying these philosophies to my life with Patrice, and beyond."

— *Von Decarlo*

ABOUT THE AUTHOR

Von Decarlo, a multi-talented performer and entertainment professional, and comedian Patrice O'Neal spent ten years together. They were best friends, lovers, and most of all, partners. Patrice's work was often inspired by this brutally honest and outside of the box relationship. Likewise, Von's work is influenced by the immense insight into men and relationships she garnered from her life with Patrice, utilizing her experiences as a relationship expert on both television and radio, as well as live appearances. Von also produced Patrice's two comedy albums: Mr. P and Unreleased and produced the music for his one hour Comedy Central special, Elephant In The Room.

"All you really have in this life is hope."

— *Patrice O'Neal*